COMPASSION
AS OUR
Compass

20+
Professional Learning Activities
to Nurture Educator Empathy

GLORIA L. CANADA

Solution Tree | Press

a division of
Solution Tree

555 North Morton Street
Bloomington, IN 47404
800.733.6786 (toll free) / 812.336.7700
FAX: 812.336.7790

email: info@SolutionTree.com
SolutionTree.com

Visit **go.SolutionTree.com/teacherefficacy** to download the free reproducibles in this book.

Printed in the United States of America

Library of Congress Cataloging-in-Publication Data
Names: Canada, Gloria L., author.
Title: Compassion as our compass : 20+ professional learning activities to
    nurture educator empathy / Gloria L. Canada.
Description: Bloomington, IN : Solution Tree Press, [2023] | Includes
    bibliographical references.
Identifiers: LCCN 2023024244 (print) | LCCN 2023024245 (ebook) | ISBN
    9781958590270 (paperback) | ISBN 9781958590287 (ebook)
Subjects: LCSH: Reflective teaching. | Teacher-student relationships. |
    Compassion. | Empathy.
Classification: LCC LB1025.3 .C356 2023 (print) | LCC LB1025.3 (ebook) |
    DDC 371.14/4--dc23/eng/20230821
LC record available at https://lccn.loc.gov/2023024244
LC ebook record available at https://lccn.loc.gov/2023024245

Solution Tree
Jeffrey C. Jones, CEO
Edmund M. Ackerman, President

Solution Tree Press
President and Publisher: Douglas M. Rife
Associate Publishers: Todd Brakke and Kendra Slayton
Editorial Director: Laurel Hecker
Art Director: Rian Anderson
Copy Chief: Jessi Finn
Senior Production Editor: Tonya Maddox Cupp
Copy Editor: Mark Hain
Proofreader: Mark Hain
Text and Cover Designer: Rian Anderson
Acquisitions Editor: Hilary Goff
Assistant Acquisitions Editor: Elijah Oates
Content Development Specialist: Amy Rubenstein
Associate Editor: Sarah Ludwig
Editorial Assistant: Anne Marie Watkins

ACKNOWLEDGMENTS

I'd like to acknowledge and thank North East ISD in San Antonio, Texas, the school district that "raised" me from a young teacher into an educational leader.

Solution Tree Press would like to thank the following reviewers:

Tonya Alexander
English Teacher (NBCT)
Owego Free Academy
Owego, New York

Jennifer Evans
Principal
Burnham School
Cicero, Illinois

John D. Ewald
Educator, Consultant, Presenter,
Coach
Retired Superintendent, Principal,
Teacher
Frederick, Maryland

Nathalie Fournier
French Immersion Teacher
Prairie South School Division
Moose Jaw, Saskatchewan, Canada

Kelly Hilliard
Mathematics Teacher
McQueen High School
Reno, Nevada

Erin Kruckenberg
Fifth-Grade Teacher
Harvard Community Unit School
District 50
Harvard, Illinois

Visit **go.SolutionTree.com/teacherefficacy** to download the free reproducibles in this book.

TABLE OF CONTENTS

Reproducibles are in italics.

DEDICATION

For my grandparents, Manuel and Petra Jimenez, who proved that anything is possible.

For my parents, Charles (Tony) and Rosa Canada, whose strong shoulders I stand upon.

For my grown sons, Charles and Eric, who inspire me to be a better human.

And for my husband, Tom, who has cheered me on to the finish line from his favorite yellow lawn chair in Little Compton, Rhode Island.

ABOUT THE AUTHOR

 **Gloria L. Canada, EdD,** is the founder of Circles of Purpose, an educational consulting company whose work focuses primarily on school leadership, family engagement, and poverty awareness. Her determination and commitment to improving schools so they respond to students' needs, support acceptance for all, and establish a belief in maintaining high expectations have resulted in substantial improvement on various campuses. Dr. Canada is also an adjunct professor for the University of Texas at San Antonio, where she teaches graduate courses in educational administration and school leadership.

Dr. Canada has been an educator since 1983. She spent twelve years as a successful Title I principal in San Antonio, where she led the campus to consistently reach a Recognized status by the Texas Educational Agency. She also served as a Professional Service Provider, working closely with principals of struggling campuses in the state of Texas. Her educational experiences have provided her with a strong background in working with predominantly low-income schools with diverse populations. Prior to becoming a school administrator, she spent ten years as a classroom teacher.

Dr. Canada is the author of a children's book, *My Hero Doesn't Wear a Cape*, which captures the essence of her childhood growing up in a military family. She has discussed this book and presented it to children at various schools and at a conference of counselors, and she was invited by the Gold Star Families organization (for families who have lost a parent, spouse, or child to war) to share a reading of her book at one of their annual gatherings.

Dr. Canada received a bachelor's degree in education from the University of Mary Hardin-Baylor in Belton, Texas, a master's degree in educational leadership and policy studies from the University of Texas at San Antonio, and a doctorate in education from Texas A&M University in College Station, Texas.

To book Gloria L. Canada for professional development, contact pd@ SolutionTree.com.

INTRODUCTION

I didn't realize it at the time, but my first lesson in compassion came from my maternal grandmother. My grandparents were new migrants to the United States, did not speak English, lived in a small house on a dirt road, and had very little money. I watched my grandmother save her pennies, nickels, and dimes and tie them up in a frayed red bandana. I saw her do this routinely and I thought she must be saving up for something really special.

At five or six years old, during a day spent with my grandparents, I walked between my grandmother and my grandfather as we began our errands. My grandmother squeezed my hand tightly, "*¡Para que no te pierdas ni te lo lleven!*" (so I don't get "lost or stolen," she said in Spanish), as we crossed the bridge into Mexico to buy inexpensive groceries. Once over the bridge, my grandparents talked with a desperately poor woman who was sitting on the hot sidewalk, holding on to her crying baby and young toddler. The mom and toddler were shoeless, dirty, and quiet. (As a child, they looked very scary to me.) My grandmother's grip on my hand loosened. She pulled the frayed red bandana full of coins from her purse, untied it, and gently placed the change in the woman's hand. My grandmother bent and whispered something in Spanish to the woman.

Over the years, I witnessed this kind of scene over and over. I eventually understood my grandmother really was saving up for something special.

What my grandmother showed, among other characteristics, was compassion. When school leadership builds compassion, the act of recognizing need and showing empathy for another creates positive human connections, as well as feelings of safety, support, connectedness, respect, and trust (Ondrasek & Flook, 2020). Students need "emotional safety centered around compassion—a necessary building block to create the positive conditions required for deep learning" (Tischio, 2021). Without compassion, there is no emotional safety, and without that feeling, a person cannot learn (Ondrasek & Flook, 2020). Creating a culture that encourages compassion and results in emotional safety may be intimidating to consider trying, but as renowned American anthropologist Margaret Mead said, "Never doubt that a small group of thoughtful, committed citizens can change the world: indeed, it's the only thing that ever has" (as cited in Keys, 1982, p. 79). If there were ever a group of people that can impact the world this way, it is a group of determined, dedicated educators.

This book is a gentle reminder for all of how easily the practices of compassion, empathy, and inclusion can be infused into our everyday lives. Compassion and empathy are closely linked but keep in mind that "while empathy refers more generally to our ability to take the perspective of and feel the emotions of another person, compassion is when those feelings and thoughts include the desire to help" (Greater Good Magazine, n.d.).

When we begin modeling compassion in our schools, we are teaching students how to be kinder human beings. The need for empathy, compassion, inclusion, and real-life human connection has never been stronger. From a worldwide pandemic to politics to bitter arguments over the correctness of what to teach and what not to teach, we see the trauma and stress these have caused not only among strangers but also within circles of friends and family. The shadowy feelings of divisiveness, judgment, and exclusion tend to permeate our everyday life. Tempers can be quick, patience short, and compassion forgotten.

Bringing compassion into schools is not only beneficial to students, but to adults as well. Licensed clinical psychologist Beth Kurland (2019) states:

> Some of the many benefits to the person expressing compassion include reduced levels of cellular inflammation, increased perceptions of happiness and an experience of pleasure, a buffering effect against stress, an increase in longevity, a broadening ability to see a wider perspective

outside of oneself, and increasing feelings of social
connection (which in and of itself have major implications for
health and well-being).

When educators are less stressed and have increased perceptions of happiness, our students are also beneficiaries. Our emotions carry over into the classroom. This book demonstrates how compassion can intentionally be taught and learned. The included activities are for educators themselves, either in groups or as individuals, but many of the activities can be converted into classroom lessons as well.

How to Use This Book

The audience for this book includes all school administrators, teacher leaders, academic coaches, school counselors, family specialists, and social workers who coach or train others, as well as individual teachers who want to learn independently.

Through short, personal vignettes, this book reveals lessons learned mostly through the experiences of a school principal. Identifying details and overall events have been changed to allow for others who were involved to remain anonymous. Visit **go.SolutionTree.com/teacherefficacy** to access free copies of the vignettes. Engaging activities lead participants to remember their cause, curiosity, compassion, and commitment to students. These activities demonstrate the challenges faced by students and how our small actions (or inactions) as educators can greatly impact the lives of students. *Intentional awareness* serves as a compass toward honest conversation, thoughtful reflection, and relationship building.

The supportive, empathy-building activities focus on bringing compassion to the forefront of what we do as educators. They allow educators precious pockets of time dedicated to sharing personal experiences, listening to others' stories, establishing personal connections, intentionally incorporating inclusion, acknowledging educators' powerful impact on students, and collaborating with colleagues in practicing compassion with each other and in their classrooms. Rather than approaching students in hurried frustration or a lack of understanding, this book delivers a needed option to begin honest dialogue and self-reflection in discovering answers to questions that many educators face, such as, How can we establish an atmosphere of compassion and kindness among our colleagues and within our classrooms? What invisible barriers do we unknowingly have in place that may cause feelings of exclusion to our colleagues, community, students, or student caregivers?

Flexibility in the use of this book is crucial and ensures the ability to address the vast and varying needs of all districts, campuses, or departments. Read the chapters in any order and complete the accompanying activities in a single session, or spread them out over a few sessions, depending on the time allotted. There are detailed lesson plans and materials lists for all supporting activities in each chapter. The goal is to clear an easy path to practicing compassion with our colleagues and with our students.

My hope is that this topic continues to be a consistent and continual focus throughout the school year. Take your time with this book. Don't be in a hurry. Let it sink in. My suggestion is to take on a different lesson each month, keeping compassion as our compass.

How This Book Is Organized

The following chapters provide helpful insights and infuse purposeful teaching through compassion.

- Chapter 1: Trauma must be acknowledged and met with compassion.

- Chapter 2: Caring about students means showing compassion and creating personal connections with them.

- Chapter 3: Acceptance is part of compassion.

- Chapter 4: Educators fill many roles supporting students by using compassion to build and strengthen trusting relationships.

- Chapter 5: Being the new student comes with its own challenges that require compassion from educators.

- Chapter 6: Take down invisible fences to encourage family engagement.

Each chapter includes the following features.

- An introduction to each chapter to set the stage

- A personal vignette and a summary of lessons learned along with supportive research

- Activities for professional learning, including objectives, a materials list, and steps for facilitated group or independent practice

- A short conclusion highlighting each chapter's main points

- A list of anticipated questions with helpful answers

- Reflection questions

- Tips throughout provide additional insight to customize an activity
  or to take it a step further

- Try It in the Classroom notes are included for transitioning
  the professional learning lessons into useful lessons or activities
  with students

My hope is to start the conversation around intentionally practicing compassion to build strong, supportive relationships with colleagues and students and for this book to be the entry point into regaining and cultivating compassion, empathy, and inclusion. This book's purpose is not to dive deep into divisive issues that risk driving the education community apart, but to acknowledge how complex and intertwined many of these issues are. The activities in this book lay the foundation for creating a path to begin this work.

CHAPTER 1
Acknowledging Trauma

Unless someone like you cares a whole awful lot,
nothing is going to get better. It's not.

—DR. SEUSS

Educators see traumatized students walk through their classroom doors daily, which makes trauma a vital concept for us to understand. *Trauma* is a group of psychological and physical "symptoms that a person might develop after going through a very frightening or upsetting experience" (Sheldon-Dean, 2022). Sometimes, a trauma is singular, though "the experience may not always be one distinct event" (Sheldon-Dean, 2022). One report shows that more than half of children in the world have experienced trauma (Hillis, Mercy, Amobi, & Kress, 2016); a 2022 report from the World Health Organization relays that that is almost one billion children. Because of trauma's prevalence in children, teachers interact closely with many students who have experienced it, and because of that, "a secondary type of trauma, known as vicarious trauma, is a big risk" for teachers (Minero, 2017).

In *Helping Children Succeed: What Works and Why*, author Paul Tough (2016) notes that "teachers convey to their students deep messages—often implicitly or even subliminally—about belonging, connection, ability, and opportunity." Wearing blinders and going through the same motions day after day is a real danger if teachers become an island, work alone, and no longer feel the power and purpose of teaching.

Students interpret what isn't spoken out loud. Are you standing with arms open and a smile on your face? Are you sitting behind your desk and expressionless as students enter the room? A simple nod of the head or the raising of an eyebrow can indicate acceptance or disapproval. Perception is important. Intentionally being aware of body language that promotes support and understanding goes a long way in establishing trust. Waving, offering a high-five, giving a knowing wink, or smiling are easy adjustments to make. Medical doctor David Rakel (2018) explains that "nonverbal cues carry more than four times the weight of verbal messages" and that while "the average person may command a vocabulary of 30,000—60,000 words, we humans rely on 750,000 nonverbal signals much more quickly and accurately than words" (p. 167). What messages are you inadvertently sending to students? The following vignette is a reminder of the importance of being intentionally aware of students' circumstances, including trauma.

But I Gave Him a Coat

"Good morning, Dr. Jergins!" says Ms. Bromo, the data processor, to the principal. Dr. Jergins has just returned from her daily morning campus walk. "I was reviewing attendance and thought you may want to know about Brandon. He enrolled three months ago and has already accumulated eighteen absences."

"Eighteen? Whose class is he in?" Dr. Jergins asks.

"He is in Mrs. Clower's, our new fifth-grade teacher's class."

"Thank you for letting me know, Ms. Bromo," says Dr. Jergins, and she leaves a note in Mrs. Clower's mailbox asking her to drop by the office when she has a minute.

Later in the day, when the two have time to meet, Dr. Jergins asks if there is anything the teacher can tell her about Brandon.

"I noticed he didn't have a coat, so I gave him one that my son had outgrown. He was appreciative."

"That was thoughtful of you. Can you tell me about his eighteen absences?"

"Yes, he is absent quite a bit. I didn't realize it was that many times," Mrs. Clower says.

"What did his mom say when you called to find out why he's been out so much?"

"No one answered my call, so I left a message asking her to call me back. No one returned my call."

"Have you communicated with the counselor to see if she knows what's going on?"

"No, I haven't. I didn't realize this would be something I would contact the counselor about."

"Does the family specialist know, so you both could do a home visit to check on the family?"

Mrs. Clower explains that she hadn't met the family specialist yet and was unsure of that person's role.

Dr. Jergins requests that Mrs. Clower reach out to either the counselor or family specialist so they can discover the reason for the absences, and says, "A home visit would be a great way to show this new family we care."

"I will, but I want you to know I really do care. I gave him a coat," she replies again.

"Thank you, Mrs. Clower. I appreciate your kindness to Brandon. However, it is very clear to me that I need to do a better job informing our new teachers of the processes and resources we have to reach out to our students and families in need. I will make a note to include this as part of our new teacher orientation sessions next year."

The following afternoon, at Brandon's house, Mrs. Clower and the school counselor are greeted by Brandon's mother. She holds a toddler on her hip and is dressed in wrinkled pajamas.

"Please come in, but excuse the mess," the young mom says. "I just started chemo and don't have the energy right now."

"That must make it difficult to get Brandon to school," offers Mrs. Clower.

"Yes, some mornings are really hard. My husband leaves for work very early, before it's time to wake up Brandon. Since we're new in town, we don't have anyone else to lean on."

"I have an idea!" states Mrs. Clower. "Two other students in my class live in this same neighborhood. How would you feel about having their parents reach out to you? Maybe they could bring Brandon to school when they bring their own kids in the mornings."

Brandon's mother says, "Thank you. I would love that."

As the women say their goodbyes, Brandon's mom stops to say, "Oh, Brandon came home from school with a new coat last week. Do you know who gave it to him?"

"I gave him a coat," says Mrs. Clower, with a grin on her face.

This story provides an example of seeing only the visible part of a problem and ignoring the potentially bigger issues underneath, such as trauma. Trauma can influence students' ability to focus and learn, and a teacher's understanding "allows them to establish trusting relationships with their students, counter negative messages that students have internalized about themselves, and create positive, accepting learning environments" (Ondrasek & Flook, 2020). When educators build such relationships, their students feel seen and heard. Their strengths and struggles are recognized. Indeed, "there is no element more critical for school success than for a staff to believe and behave in a manner that models a student-first mindset" (Casas, 2017).

Teachers are not only content educators, but they are also mentors, counselors, nurses, quasi-parents, data evaluators, and cheerleaders. Teaching is both physically and emotionally taxing, but it is also inspiring and rewarding. Being an educator takes heart. Infusing compassion into our work is our heart in action. In *Essential Truths for Principals*, authors Danny Steele and Todd Whitaker (2019) write that:

> When we are able to recenter on why we chose education,
> when we recall some of our most positive outcomes,
> when we reflect on the difference we make every day, that
> mountain can quickly become more climbable. And the hike
> is worth it. (p. 55)

When students are seen, teaching is approached with positive intentions, connections, and relationships. It is positive, caring relationships with students that confirm the undeniable magical power of teachers.

Try It in the Classroom

Occasionally have students complete a quick fill-in-the-blank form. It takes only minutes to create two or three fill-in-the-blank statements. Student responses will provide insight into what is currently important in their lives.

Think about completing the same fill-in-the-blank statement as your students and reading your statements out loud to the class. Sharing this may feel a bit vulnerable at first, but it is amazing how excited students are to see the human side of their teachers. Being vulnerable—in a way appropriate for the classroom—lets students know that they don't have to be perfect in order to achieve (Huddy, 2015), and "engaging students interpersonally increases student learning and increases the impact of the teaching" (Lowrie, 2019).

Example: If I had the power to change _____, it would make my life happier. Sometimes, I find myself wondering about _____.

Why We Need to Acknowledge Trauma

When we acknowledge the human experience of trauma (a major event a person has experienced and its impact left on the person physically and mentally), we intentionally seek to understand. It provides us with a clearer lens for understanding and communicating. Trauma can display itself in the following ways:

- Frequently thinking about, dreaming about, or acting out the traumatic event
- Feeling numb, having trouble focusing, and struggling to connect with other people
- Getting annoyed easily, acting constantly fearful or hypervigilant, or having trouble sleeping (Sheldon-Dean, 2022, p. 5)

Trauma can happen to any of us. No one is immune from the possibility of violence (being a victim of or witnessing it), neglect, or not having our needs met. We can counter the adversity that trauma brings with compassion, since "positive, stable relationships—when adults have the awareness, empathy, and cultural competence to understand and listen to children—can buffer the effects of even serious adversity" (Flook, 2019).

Exposure to an incident or series of events that are emotionally disturbing or life-threatening can have lasting adverse effects on a person's functioning and mental, physical, social or emotional well-being. *Post-traumatic stress disorder* (*PTSD*) is also recognized as a response to a wide range of disturbing or life-threatening events, including interpersonal or sexual violence, abuse, war, natural disasters, and serious accidents. You don't have to have experienced these events yourself to have PTSD; you can have witnessed them (Sheldon-Dean, 2022). Remember, also,

that individuals handle trauma in different ways. Some tend to build a wall around themselves and try to go undetected, while others become angry and lash out; common feelings include "denial, anger, fear, sadness, shame, confusion, anxiety, depression, numbness, guilt, and hopelessness, [as well as] irritability or difficulty concentrating" (Leonard, 2020). Understanding that a person's behavior may be a survival strategy can help us react with compassion rather than judgment, and training for how to help students through that trauma is crucial (Alisic, Bus, Dulack, Pennings, & Splinter, 2012).

Here are some lessons learned.

- **Truly know our students matter:** The specific action of "compassion has been identified as a promising construct for frontline professionals (teachers) in terms of promoting psychological well-being, and increasing the sensitivity to detect, tolerate and respond to distress in others" (O'Toole & Dobutowitsch, 2022). Understanding what makes each person unique from the rest takes time and intentional effort. A simple informal survey of students to get to know individual students' likes, dislikes, and special interests is one such effort that works for all grade levels. You can do the survey verbally or in written form, depending on the participants' abilities. Other research-backed strategies and activities are available in books and online, such as the resources at https://edut.to/3pGb3Ed on Edutopia. Visiting one of the lessons from this book each month helps ensure this focus is a continual source of conversation among staff.

- **Avoid making assumptions:** Have you ever prematurely judged someone harshly and then, after having the chance to get to know them better (whether in a work environment or socially), changed your opinion of them? To help avoid assumptions, we must first get to know our students, "taking an interest in their lives outside of school, learning about the challenges they face, how they learn, and what their hopes and dreams are" (Noguera, 2019).

- **Keep assumptions in check:** Ask yourself if you have used all the resources at your disposal and asked the right questions of the right people to understand a student's story. Consider using the Assumptions activity (page 15). Students of almost any age can keep a journal that they share with their teacher. In it, they can draw or write. Use a thought, question, or statement as the prompt for each journal entry. Here are two examples: Who do you consider the most important people in your life and why? What would keep you from truly reaching your dream?

- **Build relationships through empathy and compassion:** Teacher empathy and compassion benefit everyone and "can promote the development of students and the professional growth of teachers" (Ge, Li, Chen, Kayani, & Qin, 2021). Trauma and compassion go hand in hand, since "compassion has three parts: (1) feeling another's pain, (2) understanding others, and (3) desiring to help others. Compassion, and leading with passion, is a core part of mindful leadership" (Lesser, 2019). *Empathy,* explains director of the Social Neuroscience Lab at Stanford University Jamil Zaki (as cited in K.N.C., 2019), "is our ability to share and understand one another's feelings." Keep in mind that the kind of empathy you show matters, as some types actually have a negative effect. An *other-oriented response* is a "cognitive style of perspective taking where someone imagines another person's perspective, reads their emotions, and can understand them in general," and it most benefits both the person who empathizes and the person they empathize with (Konrath, as cited in Abramson, 2021). This book's activities help guide efforts toward nurturing empathy and compassion.

- **Look for this strength from someone on your campus, team, or department and follow that person's lead:** Look for those who are good listeners, who intuit how others are feeling and ask about them, and who display vulnerability (Cherry, 2023). Ask if you can have open conversations, ask questions, and learn from them. Be aware of those who *trauma dump,* or overshare to the detriment of others (Dubin, 2022). That is not the same as vulnerability. If you do not find someone on your campus who you think you can learn from, ask your supervisor for recommendations. Most supervisors have a pretty long list of associates and colleagues who they hold in high esteem and have learned from or have been mentored by over the years.

The more we learn and know about our students, their backgrounds, and their families, the more we can understand, connect, and build relationships.

Activities for Identifying and Acknowledging Trauma

The activities in this chapter focus on being intentional about knowing our students. Knowing their truth allows us to stop making assumptions (acknowledging and getting past our biases) and give those who are traumatized the support they need in the classroom.

Trauma Indicators

The following activity is centered around identifying trauma. Some signs of trauma may be physically visible, like bruises, lack of personal hygiene, and a generally negative perspective, but many signs are invisible, such as disassociating from reality and negative outlook (Sheldon-Dean, 2022).

Objective: To identify types of trauma students may be experiencing and emphasize the need for building trusting relationships.

Materials: Reproducibles "But I Gave Him a Coat" (visit **go.SolutionTree .com/teacherefficacy** to access a reproducible version of this chapter's vignette), "Risks of Trauma" (page 22), and "Causes and Consequences of Student Trauma" (page 23)

Directions for facilitated group practice follow.

1. Read aloud the "But I Gave Him a Coat" vignette from the start of this chapter.

2. Ask participants if they have ever had a student who suffered from trauma. *Without identifying students*, choose two or three teachers to share what these students were experiencing and how it affected their learning or behavior at school.

3. Pair participants and give each team one copy of the "Risks of Trauma" reproducible (page 22).

4. Have participants write, inside the blank body, possible causes and consequences of trauma.

5. Have teams take turns sharing only one trauma on their list with the whole group. As they name a trauma, participants draw a line through that word on their own sheet if they had also identified it. Each sequential team will read only one trauma they have listed that has not yet been crossed off. Continue circling through every team until all listed traumas are called out.

6. Pass out one copy of the "Causes and Consequences of Student Trauma" reproducible (page 23) to each team. Provide time for participants to compare it with the one they just created. Participants may name additional issues that cause trauma and add these to their completed body. Remind participants to keep this completed activity handy to refer to as one reminder of why compassion is necessary in schools every day. Thank your team for sharing their personal experiences with you.

7. Ask participants to look at their reproducible and share what other issues can cause trauma and if any causes or consequences surprised them. Remind participants that students are not made from cookie cutters. Every single one is different and has a story. Do you know your students' stories?

Directions for independent practice follow.

1. Read the "But I Gave Him a Coat" vignette.

2. Recall a former or current student (or even another student you knew when you were a child) who suffered from trauma. Write down what that student was experiencing and how it affected their learning or behavior in your classroom.

3. Using the reproducible "Risks of Trauma," write possible causes and consequences of trauma.

4. Compare your outline with the "Causes and Consequences of Student Trauma" reproducible. What additional issues can trauma cause? Did any causes listed surprise you?

Keep this completed activity handy to refer to later during the Reflection activity at the end of this section (page 17).

Assumptions

This activity helps expose the negative biases or beliefs that may come up when making assumptions or having conscious or unconscious biases about groups of people. Former teacher and principal Brianne Dotson (as cited in Vazquez, 2022) says this about the type of processing that takes place in this activity:

> Interrogating the information and experiences that led us to form those thoughts and behaviors can be uncomfortable, but is imperative in mitigating unconscious bias. And because unconscious bias depends on quick decisions,

slowing down and giving ourselves opportunities to question our thoughts, beliefs, and ideas before taking action is an important strategy.

Building relationships with individuals reduces the risk of assuming something about a group of students. Having uncomfortable conversations about hidden biases may have its pitfalls, since declaring why one agrees or disagrees can reveal biases or prejudices. These unconscious biases "can influence us even when they are in direct opposition to our espoused beliefs—and sometimes in opposition to our own lived experience. That's because unconscious biases are just that—unconscious" (Fiarman, 2016, p. 10). However, not having these conversations at all is the antithesis of how to address the resulting inequities. Stretching our ideas, looking at things from a different angle, and holding ourselves and others accountable can be an uncomfortable process, but necessary to learning and growing.

Objective: To examine how assumptions about students can affect student learning and relationship building and to reflect on personal experiences.

Materials: Reproducible "Assumptions" (page 24)

Directions for facilitated group practice follow.

1. Break into groups of four and provide each group with one copy of the "Assumptions" reproducible.

2. Instruct each group to read the list of assumptions and give them fifteen minutes to discuss how each assumption may affect student learning and relationship building. Each person in the small group shares why they agree or disagree with each assumption. Remind participants this is a safe learning environment where they can be honest and vulnerable.

3. The groups tally each assumption with the number of agrees or disagrees. For example, each member responds to assumption one, and someone in the group tallies responses; each member responds to assumption two, and someone tallies responses. Continue through the list until all assumptions have been discussed. Groups may add to the assumptions during discussions at their tables.

4. Debrief this activity by discussing which biases the group found most surprising. The takeaway is to understand everyone's life experiences are different. What we know to be true in our own life may not be true in someone else's life.

Directions for independent practice follow.

1. Read and mark the "Assumptions" reproducible.

2. Tally the agree and disagree for each assumption. Think about how each assumption could affect student learning and relationship building. Be honest and vulnerable.

3. Ask yourself why you hold this assumption. What other assumptions can you add to the list? What assumptions can you take away? The takeaway here is we cannot assume to know others' living situations. As a personal reflection, how would these assumptions have applied to you when you were ten years old?

Keep this completed activity handy to refer to when considering the reflection questions at the end of this chapter (page 21).

Reflection

This activity provides an introspective opportunity to internalize personal takeaways about the impact making assumptions has on others. We do not know someone's story unless they are willing to trust us enough to share it. Build trust with students with empathic listening, which "means listening to what a student has to say—a student's 'strong emotions and painful experiences'. . . and not responding. No reassuring, no offering advice. Just listening" (Marcus, as cited in Cacciatore, 2021). This is a process we can all begin to practice. The next time an adult or student says they want to talk, try the practice of empathic listening.

This activity partly depends on having participated in the Trauma Indicators (page 14) and Assumptions (page 15) activities.

Objective: To identify one significant item learned from this lesson and express why it is personally important.

Materials: Two blank index cards (to copy and complete the two printed reflection statements listed with step 2), completed reproducible "Assumptions" (page 24) from that activity, and completed reproducible "Risks of Trauma" (page 22) from the Trauma Indicators activity

Directions for facilitated group practice follow.

1. Ask participants to place their completed "Risks of Trauma" and completed "Assumptions" reproducibles in front of them and spend one minute thinking about the conversations that took place during

those activities. I have found it adds to the calmness of the room to have soft music playing during this reflection time.

2. After one minute, ask participants to write and fill in the blanks in the following sentences on their own index cards (one statement per card). They do not need to write their name on the card. Without names, participants are more likely to be more open with their responses.

   - *Something I will remember from today is* _____.
   - *It is important to me because* _____.

3. When most participants finish, have them tape their cards on a display wall or large poster board.

4. Center the debrief conversation on understanding how others' lives can often be very different from our own personal experiences. Understanding this provides background context for the importance of getting to know the worlds our students live in. Truly getting to know someone takes intention.

5. After the meeting, type all the reflection responses and email all of them to the participants. Try to do so no later than the end of the following week. Allowing participants the opportunity to read all responses will provide them insight into the group's learning and thinking.

Directions for independent practice follow.

1. Review your completed "Risks of Trauma" and completed "Assumptions" reproducibles.

2. Set a timer for one minute and think about the impact each trauma indicator may have on a student.

3. After one minute, write and complete the following two sentences on an index card.

   - *Something I will remember from this activity is* _____.
   - *It is important to me because* _____.

4. Keep this card in a prominent place (but away from students) as a visual reminder to recognize invisible trauma. Keep in mind that some seemingly undesirable behaviors are the result of trauma and beg for compassionate responses.

Next Steps

Identifying trauma-based and hard-to-see needs and practicing compassion with everyone, but especially with those who seem to struggle the most (or have us struggling the most), is part of addressing those needs. But reflecting must be tied to action, as the most effective unconscious bias "teaches attendees to manage their biases, change their behavior, and track their progress. It gives them information that contradicts stereotypes" (Gino & Coffman, 2021).

Common Questions

Three common questions show up when acknowledging student trauma: (1) What if a student does not want to share with me? (2) As a teacher, how do I respond to a student sharing something disturbing with me? and (3) When can I find time specifically for empathy in my packed day?

What If a Student Does Not Want to Share With Me?

It takes a great deal of vulnerability to trust someone. If you have shown empathy and compassion, someone is more likely to open up, but the issue may be extremely private or embarrassing to them.

- Assure them you will not think less of them or their family.

- If they remain closed off, don't give up. Continue to show you care and are concerned.

- Seek them out to ask how they've been doing when you see them.

- If you suspect you know what the problem is and experienced a similar rough patch at their age, share your experience, if appropriate.

- Always offer the guidance of a school counselor or social worker if there is one on the campus. If there is not, campuses often share counselors or social workers. Arrange for them to visit with the student. Many counselors can provide hotline numbers.

How Do I Respond to a Student Sharing Something Disturbing With Me?

If a student shares something with you that is disturbing, share it with your supervisor and counselor as soon as you can.

- Remain calm and let the student know you want them to be safe.

- Move to a private space (away from where others can hear).

- Listen and paraphrase.

- Let the student know you will share the information with adults who will help.

- Tell your supervisor and follow the process and protocols provided by your campus or district.

- Although laws vary by area, most educators are mandated reporters of issues such as neglect or abuse.

- See if your district has a hotline available for students and their families to access.

Of course, immediately reach out to a professional on campus if there is a possibility of a student harming themselves or others. Do *not* keep this in confidence.

When Can I Find Time Specifically for Empathy in My Packed Day?

Showing empathy takes only minutes or seconds. Some simple ideas follow.

- Put a one-sentence note on a student's desk. This can be either an affirmation or a kind note. (For example, *Your determination is admirable! Your handwriting is so neat and easy to read! I'm happy to see you!* or *You set a great example for others!*)

- Leave a positive voicemail for the parents or guardians.

- Ask a student about his, her, or their day.

- Share a story about how you have had a similar experience.

- Recognize birthdays, milestones, or accomplishments.

Tip

Recognition takes seconds and does not have to cost a lot of money. It can be something as simple as giving someone a special pencil, snack, or note; singing "Happy Birthday"; letting someone have a homework-free day; hanging an inexpensive birthday banner; or providing a fun hat to wear in class.

Reflection Questions

Consider the following questions, perhaps with a colleague.

- What was the last act of kindness you showed to a student who was difficult to reach?

- In what ways would you benefit from knowing a student's truth, rather than believing assumptions?

- What is something people may assume about you if they do not know you well?

Risks of Trauma

Causes and Consequences of Student Trauma

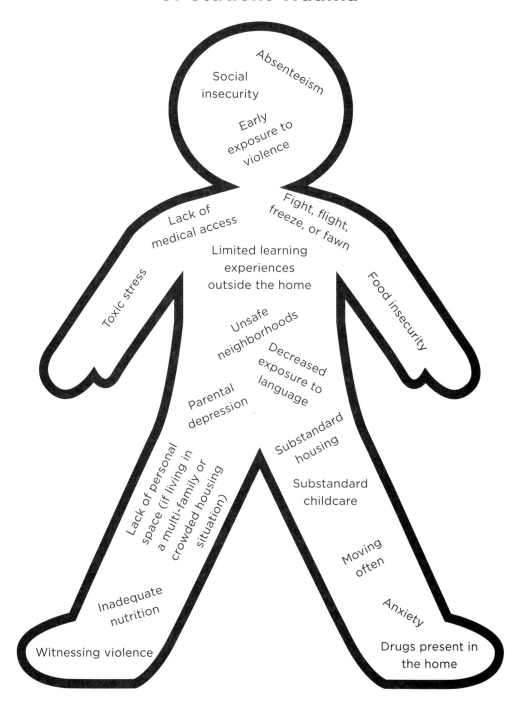

Assumptions

Each person in your group will share their experiences about why they either agree or disagree with each assumption. Tally the number of "agrees" or "disagrees" for each assumption.

Assumption	Agree	Disagree
1. Students get sufficient sleep.		
2. Students eat dinner each evening.		
3. Students eat regularly on weekends.		
4. Students who are underage have adult supervision after school.		
5. Students have basic school supplies at home.		
6. Students feel safe in their home.		
7. Students have at least one adult who cares about them.		
8. Students have shoes that fit.		
9. Students have parents who assist with homework.		
10. Students see a doctor when they are sick.		
11. Students look forward to having holidays from school.		
12. Students have visited the local attractions in their hometown.		
13. Students have reading material (books and magazines) at home.		
14. Students are made to feel special on their birthday.		
15. Parents will answer their phone when the school calls.		
16. Students trust authority (teachers, police, social workers).		
17. Students have transportation to attend before- or after-school clubs or tutoring.		

C H A P T E R   2
Creating Connections

Every child is one caring adult away from
being a success story.

—JOSH SHIPP

Finding ways to intentionally connect with students and their families demonstrates caring. In my experience, such connections have the greatest impact when developing a foundation of understanding with families. Whether a teacher, counselor, or administrator, a visit from an educator sends a family the clear message that their child is important and cared about. Such a visit can begin establishing trust:

> A trusting relationship with teachers might encourage parents to become involved in their children's education, leading to improvements in attendance, behavior, and learning. At the same time, home visits allow teachers to learn more about students' backgrounds, interests, and life experiences, which they can then draw on to improve their teaching. (Terziev, 2018)

Consider the shared history of families who have had more than one child pass through the doors of your school. You may be greeted by a student you had in school in previous years, or you may meet younger siblings who are not yet school age. Make home visits with a colleague—another teacher the student currently has, a counselor, a coach, or an administrator. The time and effort of conducting home visits turn our *feelings* of caring into *actions*.

Every day we encounter opportunities to act. Sometimes we create a plan, and sometimes things may happen by accident. Have you ever had a feeling that strongly pulls at you until you act on it? The feeling that says, *I don't know why, but I feel like I need to do this today.* The following vignette demonstrates not only the value of listening to that feeling but also acting on it. Small decisions make big impacts.

Birthday Cake

Brian entered fourth grade in the middle of the year. It was a difficult time for him, to say the least. His family had moved to Texas after a hurricane ravaged their home in New Orleans. He was angry at his mom about having to move, angry about leaving his friends, and angry about starting a new school. He didn't show much effort or interest in school. He had trouble making friends and often veered the other students' attention away from the teacher with his antics. His mom rarely answered calls from the school.

Brian began visiting the principal, Ms. Vu, in her office to complete his assignments and seemed to do better work there. Ms. Vu placed a student's desk in her office to accommodate him. Brian often asked Ms. Vu questions, and she answered him—sometimes without even looking up. Eventually, those questions turned into short conversations. On one of those days in her office, Brian had been quiet for some time. When Ms. Vu turned to glance at him, he was intently reading the school newspaper he had found lying on the chair next to him.

With the upcoming school year about to begin, Ms. Vu kept thinking about Brian. He lived in an apartment complex known for drug presence and violence. Determined to keep up their connection, she asked her assistant principal and counselor to accompany her on a home visit.

After knocking on the door, Brian swung the door open and beamed a huge grin, his confused mom in the background. Ms. Vu managed to blurt out, "Hi, we just wanted to stop by and—" when Brian interrupted with, "How did you know today was my birthday?!"

Ms. Vu thought fast. "Well, Brian, we were just on our way to the grocery store and wanted to know what kind of birthday cake you liked." The trio left and returned with a chocolate cake covered in chocolate icing, a small

box of candles, and some paper plates. Brian's mom, near tears, asked if they would like to come in and have a slice. Of course, they did! The group talked, sang, and ate chocolate cake.

The encounter in this vignette is a lesson in choosing *not* to go about business as usual, but instead taking the opportunity for an unexpected detour and sharing a gesture of kindness in an effort to connect with someone. It is a reminder that relationship building is a crucial part of our job as educators. In fact, data show that relationship building must be prioritized (Casas, 2017). A meta-analysis finds that:

strong teacher-student relationships were associated in both the short and long term with improvement on practically every measure schools care about: higher student academic engagement, attendance, grades, few disruptive behaviors and suspensions, and lower school dropout rates. Those effects were strong even after controlling for differences in students' individual, family, and school backgrounds. (Sparks, 2019)

Doing a home visit was the initial intended step for Ms. Vu. Simply visiting the student would have been enough. But Ms. Vu discovered an opportunity to do more, to slow down, and to demonstrate kindness. Years later, Brian's family may never remember a regular home visit taking place, but I can guarantee they will never forget the impromptu birthday party celebrated in their home with the school principal.

This chapter addresses the importance of creating connections and explains why it's important to emphasize positive relationship building and going the extra step with students. The activities, when executed, help serve that relationship-building purpose.

Tip

Most people love to celebrate their special day. Always keep a few boxes of blank cards in your desk. (They work for all occasions at a moment's notice.) Recognize people with small gestures.

- **School administrator:** Keep a list of staff birthdays. On their birthday (or other special day), place something in their box with a small note attached—a card, their favorite canned drink, a snack, a set of pencils, a school

pen, an early-out pass, or an offer to take over their class
for fifteen minutes to give them a well-deserved break.

- **Teachers, counselors, and family specialists:** Post
student birthdays on the wall by month (if the person
is comfortable with that since some religions do not
celebrate birthdays). Create a tradition of having the
class sing "Happy Birthday" to the person celebrating (if
they enjoy the attention); give the student a handwritten
card, a fancy pencil, a candy bar, a special chair to sit in,
or a free homework pass. These kind gestures work for
students of all ages.

Why We Need to Create Connections

Connections are critical, since "our interactions with others are crucial for the well-being of our brain, and our happiness. Because we need to conform, we need to belong, to feel safe and secure, and for our brains to work like they should" (Burnett, 2018, p. 138). If we remember one thing, it should be that every day is an opportunity to be a positive source of connection for students, and that "establishing such connections requires the ability to express care and concern for other people, as well as to identify with them" (Lonczak, 2019). In fact, students whose classrooms have compassion show more cooperation and improved learning (Lonczak, 2019).

The emotional bonds that form when people feel connected provide emotional support and security. Think of the way we feel when we are around people we have a positive connection with. We are comfortable, honest, supportive, and responsive to each other's needs. *The Power of Moments* authors Chip Heath and Dan Heath (2017) state:

> Studies show that responsive treatment leads infants to
> feel secure and children to feel supported; it makes people
> more satisfied with their friends; and it brings couples closer
> together. Responsiveness is correlated with attachment,
> self-esteem, emotional well-being, and a laundry list of other
> positive attributes. (pp. 232–233)

Self-esteem and emotional well-being are two important traits to develop in the students we teach because social-emotional intelligence is needed in every area of life. It leads to improved "relationships at home and at school, empathy, self-esteem, self-awareness, communication skills, positive thinking patterns, problem-solving, stress response, mood, and motivation" (Srakocic, 2022).

Ideas for connecting with a particular student who is struggling include scheduling a weekly (or biweekly) lunch with them, beginning a journal that goes back and forth between teacher and student, creating signals that convey positive messages or directions to the student, meeting with the parents and the student to talk about positive progress, and giving the student a meaningful book (privately and out of view of the class).

Here are some lessons learned.

- **Build relationships based on trust:** All students deserve to have at least one adult at school they know cares about them. For adult educators, having great relationships with great students is easy. Establishing great relationships with students who are struggling, who may not know the social norms, whose behavior is challenging, or who demand a lot of negative attention may not be so easy. It takes effort: "Learning about our students requires work and commitment. Stereotypes and assumptions about children or the communities where they live often get in the way. It requires a willingness to build relationships with students that are rooted in trust" (Noguera, 2019). Reach out and let these students know you care about them, since "when we practice wise compassion by bringing more of our humanity to our leadership, we can create a culture in which others increase their focus on real human connections" (Hougaard & Carter, 2021). This rings true even if we make mistakes, as former educator and speaker Jimmy Casas (2017) explains: "Approach each situation with an understanding that at the heart of every problem is a conversation to be had" (p. 44). Communication with colleagues is key.

- **When caregivers know you care about their children, walls come down:** Brian's mother, who did not return phone calls and often managed to avoid school personnel, hugged school personnel because of a simple unplanned act of kindness toward her child. This became the impetus of a trusting relationship with this family. The kindness helped establish some trust in her for the staff, and "Trust is a crucial factor in parent–teacher relationships" (Schweizer, Niedlich, Adamczyk, & Bormann, 2017, p. 97).

- **Practice gratitude instead of taking things for granted:**
  Teaching, counseling, and social work are humbling acts of service
  and purpose. However, the proximity we have to students who are
  experiencing abuse, neglect, poverty, consistent moves, or other
  trauma can jar us into gratitude. Put that gratitude and compassion
  to good use; they "make us more willing to cooperate with and invest
  in others" (DeSteno, 2018).

Tip

When you find yourself a little embarrassed by all you take
for granted, admit your error and then do something to make
a difference. Little efforts can lead to big changes. Consider
these suggestions.

- If you are an administrator, provide a small (but hugely
  appreciated) act of kindness by occasionally covering a
  teacher's class for fifteen minutes and giving the teacher
  an unexpected break.

- Remember a colleague's birthday and cover their
  duty for the day.

- Make a few extra sack lunches and ask a couple of
  students to dine with you in the classroom. You might
  do this on a rotating basis to ensure all your students
  experience the treat of having lunch with the teacher.

- Tape individualized encouraging notes to students' desks
  the morning before a test.

- Create a poem—it doesn't have to rhyme!—that includes
  each student's name and state what about them you are
  grateful for.

These small acts of kindness that demonstrate gratitude
and compassion are not difficult to do, and "of all the ways
we can create moments of pride for others, the simplest
is to offer them recognition" (Heath & Heath, 2017, p. 145).
Be creative and brainstorm with your team, grade-level
colleagues, or department to think of ways to show students
you care. You'll be amazed at the ideas that emerge from
your brainstorming session.

Activities for Creating Connections

Let us not be so busy teaching, planning, grading, and meeting that we lose focus on what is ultimately important: the students as whole beings. Remember to look for and attempt to truly see those who are in our classrooms. What do we know about the students we serve? Who is the person with the constant smile or the one with the ill-fitting clothes, the head asleep on the desk, the constant talker, the expressionless student, or one who tries to make everyone laugh?

The following activities focus on the importance of intentionally taking the time to look at students as individuals. The challenges and struggles students carry with them are unique and part of their personal story. Knowing the students we teach, who they are, and where they come from forces us to see them as individuals rather than as a class. The lesson here is to ensure we truly see our students and to be that caring adult, that protective factor, at school who ensures students succeed (Longobardi, Prino, Marengo, & Settanni, 2016).

Do You Know Me?

This activity focuses on the intentionality of opening the door, reaching across, and making connections. Whether it's people we work with or students we teach, the more we get to know someone, the stronger the connection we form, and for children, this person is often a teacher: "Just one relationship with a caregiver throughout a lifespan can actually change the brain's development, heal trauma and promote learning" (Cacciatore, 2021).

Objective: To identify struggling students who need a personal connection, to identify their positive attributes, to reach out and intentionally connect with them.

Materials: Colored pencils, the "Birthday Cake" vignette (page 36), and the reproducible "Do You Know Me?" (page 37)

Directions for facilitated group practice follow.

1. Read aloud the "Birthday Cake" vignette from the start of this chapter.

2. Ask the participants to close their eyes and picture all the students they work with for about ten seconds.

3. Ask them to choose one student who needs special attention—emotionally, socially, academically, or otherwise. It can be the student who often goes unnoticed.

4. Ask participants to spend ten seconds picturing this student. What facial expressions, body language, physical appearance, attitude, and words do they see when they think of this student?

5. Pass out "Do You Know Me?" and colored pencils. Ask participants to spend five minutes drawing the student (including details such as earrings, headband, and glasses).

6. Provide guidance to participants by reading aloud page 2 of "Do You Know Me?" Invite participants to share other suggestions, comments, ideas, or experiences.

7. After the discussion, ask participants to complete the prompts at the bottom of their sheet.

8. Break into groups of four. Share and discuss each person's individual commitment of the week, as well as offer ideas. The length of this discussion is determined by the amount of time available. The group discussion should focus on two things: (1) how much individual participants felt they knew about the student they chose or how little they knew and (2) the teacher's goal for intentionally getting to know this student better. If time permits, the group can brainstorm ideas to use in the classroom that focus on relationship building.

Directions for independent practice follow.

1. Read the "Birthday Cake" vignette.

2. Close your eyes and picture all the students you work with. Choose one student who needs special attention emotionally, socially, academically, or otherwise.

3. Picture this student in your mind. What facial expressions, body language, physical appearance, attitude, and words do you see when you think of this student?

4. Spend five minutes drawing the student (including details such as earrings, headband, and glasses).

5. Were you able to visualize this student clearly or was the image one of an "invisible" student who tends to shrink away in class? Make the commitment to do something for this student.

Creating Connections

This activity entails teachers doing something, in writing, directly for the students they teach. There is something special about receiving a handwritten note from someone. It is not a rushed email or a quick pat on the back. The effort and thought behind this gesture speak of caring.

Discount stores often carry a variety of packages containing about six notecards. Choosing a variety of cards is ideal.

Objective: To create a positive connection with a student through note writing.

Materials: Blank greeting cards with envelopes, (optional) stamps, and reproducible "Creating Connections: Starter Samples" (page 40)

Directions for facilitated group practice follow.

1. Pass out "Creating Connections: Starter Samples" and two or three blank greeting cards to each participant.

2. Identify a student or caregiver who may need some compassion.

3. Write a positive note to them, mentioning something specific that can create or reaffirm a connection.

4. As participants finish their cards, debrief by asking how participants felt as the writer. Did writing these kind messages to students come naturally or did it take some concentration and effort? Discuss how they think the recipients will feel. What reaction will the student's caregivers have when they read the kind words from the teacher to their child? There is a good chance the student is not the only one who will find joy in the card. This activity may also help develop a more positive relationship between the teacher and the student's family. If time permits, ask a couple of participants to share a time they received an unexpected note and what it meant to them.

5. The teacher can give the card to the student or can mail the card to the student's home.

Directions for independent practice follow.

1. Identify a student or caregiver who may need some compassion.

2. Write a positive note to them, mentioning something specific that can create or reaffirm a connection. Read "Creating Connections: Starter Samples" for ideas if you need some.

3. Give the card to the student or mail the card to the student's home.

4. Think about the last time you received an unexpected note from a friend, colleague, or relative. Who was it from, and what did it mean to you?

Try It in the Classroom

You can easily adapt the Creating Connections activity for students in K–12. Have students write kind notes to either classmates, an adult on campus, or a family member. Brainstorm reasons to feel grateful for, compliment, or recognize people.

Tip

Getting mail via the post office is a rare occurrence for students—for anyone, really! For a student, to receive a letter addressed to them personally is a big deal. If possible, put a stamp on it and mail your note.

Next Steps

Be prepared for relationship building to take time and effort. With students who require more time or effort to reach, it is even more important that educators connect. Connections build trust over time. It is important to remember that "children who have been neglected or abused have problems forming relationships with teachers, a necessary first step in a successful classroom experience. They've learned to be wary of adults, even those who appear to be reliable" (Miller, 2023). Be patient as you intentionally develop relationships with students and families. It will yield positive rewards. These relationships develop trust and often raise self-confidence in students, showing students they are important and seen. Relationship building with both students and their parents matters.

Common Questions

Two common questions show up around connection creation: (1) What if I have tried everything and can't build rapport with a student? and (2) How is establishing trust with the student's family beneficial?

What If I've Tried Everything and Can't Build Rapport With a Student?

Being consistent can pay off.

- **Don't rush it:** Developing relationships happens in small steps. Don't quit reaching out to the student.

- **Try the 2 × 10 intervention:** This research-supported relationship-building strategy has a teacher talking to a student for two minutes, ten days in a row (Greater Good in Education, n.d.; Wlodkowski, 1983). Ask open-ended questions about the student's interests instead of talking about academics or behavior.

- **Enlist a buddy teacher who is willing to be the student's mentor:** It is possible the student is feeling your frustration. Mentors make a positive difference for students (De La Rosa, 2022).

- **Ask the student what would make him, her, or them feel special:** Offer to work on this together.

- **Use the expertise of your staff to support you:** Many schools have counselors, family specialists, and coaches who may know the students (and their families) well.

- **Establish the practice of restorative circles:** This is a space for relationship building in the classroom routine (Tischio, 2021). Topics discussed during this circle time are innocuous, such as favorite foods, pets, and favorite activities. As the year progresses, use the circle to solve problems and give voice to all students.

How Is Establishing Trust With the Student's Family Beneficial?

A student's home life influences learning. As walls between schools and caregivers begin to break down:

> there is a move from information giving (on the part of the schools) to a sharing of information between parents and schools [and this sharing of information establishes] a more equitable distribution of agency with regard to children's learning, between parents and schools, to change in the relationship among all three actors in the process. (Goodall & Montgomery, 2014, as cited in McNinch, 2022, p. 54)

Visualize the actors in establishing student success as a tripod, with the three supporting legs being the school, the home, and the student themselves. The three legs working together provide the most support.

Reflection Questions

Consider the following questions, perhaps with a colleague.

- What are the possible consequences if a student remains under the radar all year?

- What small act of kindness could you do today that would make a difference for a student or a student's family?

- Can you think of a time when you could have gone that extra step for a student but didn't? What kept you from doing so? How can you eliminate that barrier?

Do You Know Me?

What personal struggles do you know about this student?

What are this student's positive attributes?

What ideas for connecting do you have?

What is your commitment this week to make a difference for this student?

page 1 of 2

Consider this guidance as you reflect and work through the Do You Know Me? activity.

Struggles:

- What evidence do you see of this student struggling? Attendance, grades, behavior, social isolation, physical appearance, and information provided from counselor or parent conferences, such as depression or self-harm, are a few items to consider.

- Do you know of an ongoing family situation? Is the family new to the area or even new to the country, is there a new baby in the family or a grandparent moving into the home, or is someone experiencing a new or long-term illness? Is the family going through a divorce, experiencing food insecurity, possible use of drugs, or is the absence of adult supervision a source of struggle?

Positive attributes:

- Everyone has strengths if we take the time to look. Does this student demonstrate strong leadership abilities or show academic strength in a particular area?

- Do they make friends easily, are they reliable when asked to do errands, or do they display acts of kindness to others? Look for things like great penmanship, keeping an organized desk, and raising their hand to answer questions.

Ideas for connecting:

- Schedule a weekly or biweekly lunch with this student.

- Begin a journal that goes back and forth between teacher and student using a spiral notebook.

- Create hand signals that convey positive messages or directions to the student.

- Meet with the parents (with the student present) to talk about positive progress.

- Give the student a book that is meaningful (privately and out of view of the class).

Creating Connections

Objective: Create a positive connection with a student through note writing.

Materials: Greeting cards with envelopes, pens or pencils, and stamps (if mailing the letters)

Directions follow.

1. Identify a student or caregiver who may need a more personal, caring connection from you.

2. Handwrite a positive note to them to begin creating a personal connection. Refer to "Creating Connections: Starter Samples" (page 40) as a guide for ideas to begin writing.

The teacher can give the card to the student or can mail the card to the student's home.

Creating Connections: Starter Samples

Dear _____,

I've noticed how nice you are to other students. I have heard you complimenting your classmates. Thank you for spreading kindness in our class.

Sincerely,

_____

Dear _____,

Thank you for always turning your work in on time. It shows me you are responsible and care about your learning. That is so important. Keep up the good work!

Sincerely,

_____

Dear _____,

Something that makes you special is how you walk your little brother to class every morning. I'm sure that must make him feel safe and loved. What a loving big sister you are!

Sincerely,

_____

Dear _____,

I want you to know how much I enjoy your sense of humor. You certainly can make me laugh! Keep smiling!

Sincerely,

_____

Dear _____,

I'm so happy you are in my class. I think you are a wonderful (kid, teenager, student, person). It is so nice to see you walk in the door every day.

Sincerely,

_____

Dear _____,

I admire you. You always try your best. You are a terrific example to other students because you never give up. Thank you.

Sincerely,

_____

Dear _____,

When your team was working on your group project, I noticed what a good listener you are. That is a great skill to have and rare to find!

Sincerely,

_____

CHAPTER 3

Accepting Others

Do not judge my story by the chapter you walked in on.

—UNKNOWN

My mom used to say, "Just because it's different doesn't make it wrong." This adage can apply to almost anything: people, food, customs, dress. As a military family, we had the opportunity to experience places, people, and things in a different way from what we considered usual.

If you are not used to connecting with others who are not like yourself, making assumptions about others might be easy. We see the world, its people, and its predicaments through our own personal lens of experience. Unknowingly, we often tend to view the actions or words of others through the lens of judgment. I know I'm guilty of shaking my head and thinking, "I don't get it. Why would that person do [say, think] that?" This is why we need to step back and remember that we all view things through the lens of our individual experiences. Let's open our lenses wide.

Consider the Golden Rule, which you can think of in these terms:

> A helpful step for putting wise compassion in action since it requires the consideration of another person's point of view. . . . We can take a moment to recognize that we have one view of the situation, but things may, and probably do, look very different from another person's perspective. (Hougaard & Carter, 2021)

In so many words, treat others how you want to be treated.

The following vignette demonstrates that in order to understand another's perspective or thought process, we must be open to listening with the intent to understand. I

call this *thoughtful listening*. It becomes easier to accept differences when we seek to understand someone else's perspective or reasoning. In doing so, acceptance begins to filter in and allows compassion to become part of the equation. In a people-oriented career, thoughtful listening is a daily event.

The Tennis Shoes

Principal Eugene is walking by the school's clinic when he pops in to say, "Hi." Nurse Amelia, her assistant, Ms. Connie, and a kindergarten student named Jack all smile in response. Principal Eugene glances at Jack's feet and notices his two big toes nearly poking out of the old tennis shoes. Clothes and shoes are obviously passed down from one of the four siblings to the next, and Jack is the youngest.

Nurse Amelia explains, "We were just telling Jack that today is his lucky day. Look what I have!" and produces a new pair of tennis shoes in his size. Jack goes back to class wearing his new shoes.

The next morning, as usual, Principal Eugene welcomes students and caregivers as they arrive at school. As Jack approaches him, he notices the boy is not wearing the shoes that he left school in the day before. Today's shoes are worn in, the shoelaces are frayed, and they are at least one size too big.

Away from the other arrivals, Principal Eugene says, "Good morning, Jack! I see you have some different shoes on. Where are the ones you got from Nurse Amelia yesterday?"

"My mom took them," says Jack, who gives Principal Eugene a high-five and skips into the building. Why would his mom have taken away his new, well-fitting shoes? Was she upset that the school gave them to him?

When Principal Eugene gets ahold of Jack's mother on the phone, she explains that she had to sell the shoes to buy groceries.

Consider Jack's language here and how it must have sounded to Principal Eugene: "My mom took them." Interpreted the wrong way, this might even sound sinister. What reason could someone have to take away this much-needed gift of shoes? Clearly, there was a reason. This vignette is a wake-up call about judging someone without first having some knowledge about what it is to be them. We are, each of us, susceptible to assuming the worst. We often make assumptions through the lens of our personal experience. After spending some time getting to know Jack's family, Principal Eugene and some of his staff were able to connect them to the right community support. The more we connect, the more we know, but it takes compassion to believe the best, not the worst. Every family has a story.

Why We Need to Accept Others

Acceptance is "related to the right and freedom of people to live as they wish as long as they do not harm other people" (Cuadrado, Ordóñez-Carrasco, López-Rodríguez, Vázquez, & Brambilla, 2021). The freedom to live as one desires can refer to many things, including religion, sexual orientation, cultural practices, or even how we raise our families. As educators, we have opportunities every day to model acceptance of such choices. We can model through our responses during class discussions, in our reactions to world events, and even when a new student enters the class. Students are watching and listening even when we may think they aren't. Are our biases showing through?

For the purpose of this book, we discuss the two types of biases described in table 3.1.

TABLE 3.1: Types of Bias

Description	Example
Unconscious bias, or *implicit bias*, is unknowingly discriminating "and stereotyping [someone] based on race, gender, sexuality, ethnicity, ability, age and so on" (Tsipursky, 2020). These "snap judgments" are "based upon years of subconscious socialization" (Harvard School of Public Health, n.d.).	A second-grade student takes books up to the low-income school's library counter to check out. The librarian, who is pleasantly familiar with the student, is absent that day. The substitute librarian looks at the books and says, "You can't check these out. They are way too hard for you. You are only in second grade." The student, who reads on a fifth-grade level, leaves without checking out any books. The substitute librarian unconsciously believes this elementary student was unlikely to be an advanced reader because of low socioeconomic status.

continued →

Description	Example
Negativity bias, which is theorized to be experienced by everyone, occurs when we "give greater weight to negative entities (e.g., events, objects, personal traits)" (Rozin & Royzman, 2001).	The second-grade student's negativity bias results in his not going back to the school library. His memory of what the substitute librarian said to him, and her attitude toward him, leads him to focus on that instead of his pleasant previous interactions with the regular librarian.

Our body language may also send a message about bias, whether unconscious or not. Psychologically, we can put up barriers or take down barriers without saying a word. We have a choice of standing with our arms folded in front of us or extending our open arms with a welcome greeting to all who enter. Folding our arms and not providing appropriate, reciprocal eye contact with our colleagues or with students as they file into class can be interpreted as wanting to keep a distance physically or emotionally (or both). On the other hand, a handshake, a wave, or a high-five welcomes and demonstrates acceptance. It says, "I see you; I welcome you; I care." Caring and compassion go hand in hand. Being aware of our body language allows us to make an intentional effort at sending positive messages.

Zen teacher and author Marc Lesser (2019) identifies two key practices that apply in this instance.

1. Notice your filters. What stories get in the way of you listening?

2. Avoid assuming you know what others feel and think. Instead, listen to learn what is currently silent to you.

Additionally, when we take the time to know the families we work with, it becomes easier to see the invisible, such as why certain caregivers rarely come on campus or why some students are excessively pushed to excel. In the case of parents or guardians rarely coming to campus, it might be easy to assume they don't care. But in getting to know families, you may discover they personally did not have a good school experience when they were young and that may cause them to detach; sometimes, a family's language is different from the main language spoken on campus and no translators are available. Or there could be an illness at home that prevents them from participating in school events. Familiarity reduces assumptions. Consider this humbling reminder by David Rakel (2018), who is chair of the University of Wisconsin's department of Family Medicine and Community Health: "The details of one's worldview can be so intrusive they may distort evidence that's plainly apparent." The choice is simple. Inclusion and acceptance are acts of compassion that become part of people's memories.

Tip

Providing personalized treats is one tiny way to spread feelings of warmth and appreciation. Provide an opportunity for each person in your department or campus to complete a form (electronic or paper) where they name some of their favorite items. Refer to this list throughout the year when wanting to recognize a colleague for any reason (or no reason at all). You can keep a binder of the cards in the front office for anyone who wants to gift someone.

The following list has the kinds of favorites you could include on the card.

- Cold drink
- Hot drink
- Snack
- Candy
- Color
- Book
- Place to shop

Try It in the Classroom

Students love the opportunity to share what their favorite things are. Have students complete a These Are a Few of My Favorite Things card about themselves. Having this information will come in handy all school year. Use the information on these cards to recognize birthdays, holidays, academic growth, or achievements of all kinds. It is a special way to show students you care about them as individuals. Consider this: a child's life "can sometimes be redirected by things that might at first seem, to the adult in their lives, to be small and insignificant . . . [but] can create powerful changes, and those individual changes can resonate on a national scale" (Tough, 2016, p. 113).

Note: If students are too young to write or are unable to complete the card themselves, simply ask them (or their caregiver) and complete the card for them.

Here are some lessons learned.

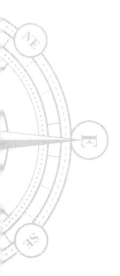

- **Make it an objective to listen and build relationships with students and parents:** In her book, *I Wish My Teacher Knew* (2016), Kyle Schwartz points out that "these objectives may not be written in curriculum manuals, but they are as essential to education as math and science" (p. 12). Education is about people first. Chapter 5 (page 87) has activities and information toward that end.

- **Do not make assumptions:** Don't only know your students' names; know their history and their stories. Poverty itself does not reveal individual family circumstances. What appears as a bad decision to some may be a good decision for a struggling family, such as Jack's in "The Tennis Shoes" vignette. Students attending schools in middle- and high-socioeconomic areas experience these difficulties as well. It may be that multiple families living together in an apartment are sharing rent and expenses. Know who your families are.

- **Mistakes can sometimes be our best teacher:** If we make deliberate decisions with the best of intentions while being mindful and compassionate of the needs of others (both our students and our colleagues), we are on the right path. In his *Forbes* magazine article, "Four Reasons Why Compassion Is Better for Humanity Than Empathy," Rasmus Hougaard (2020) writes, "Compassionate feelings, thoughts, and decisions pass through filters of consciousness, which means we can deliberate, reflect, and improve on decisions." We are human. We are always in the process of improving and growing.

- **Modeling honest conversations with colleagues about collective beliefs provides a road map to where we want to go:** Our shared purpose becomes clear when we are honest and collaborative. The time spent discussing how to create positive interactions and deepen connections with our students is time well spent. It is not fluff or frivolity. The never-ending logistics, paperwork, and mandates are important, but they're not as important as the human component. Time spent creating bonds among co-workers and students is time well spent.

Activities for Accepting and Including Others

Participants in the following activities can identify what organizers often overlook and what changes they can make to include more students and their families. For example, if a campus holds an annual fundraiser such as a Spring Fling Festival and charges an admission fee to be on the grounds, is it really for all students? More than likely, some students would love to attend but can't because the entrance fee may be an unintentional barrier. Could students earn admission to the festival? Perfect attendance for a specific length of time, being caught doing a good deed, working a shift at a booth at the festival, or volunteering a certain number of hours could all easily earn an entrance ticket.

With that in mind, and with an eye toward accepting other people, the following activities focus on having conversations with purpose. Educators' busy days don't often allow for time to share anything other than lesson plans, schedules, and working conference periods. These activities allow time for sharing and listening to the thoughts and opinions of our colleagues. The unexpected conversations that arise through these activities also provide an opportunity to look deeper into our experiences and practice.

During these activities, participants practice making decisions from another person's perspective, which is key to practicing healthy empathy (Abramson, 2021). How do you weigh your options? Who do you ask for guidance? Does one thing have to be given up for another, more important, need? Are decisions always cut and dry, good or bad?

When We Say *All*, Do We Mean All?

This activity provides a unique way to look at how inclusive school activities may or may not be for every student.

Objective: To identify school activities that may have barriers, identify the barriers, and come up with solutions to increase inclusivity.

Materials: Writing utensils and reproducibles "Eat a Good Breakfast" (page 62) and "When We Say All, Do We Mean All?" (page 63)

Directions for facilitated group practice follow.

1. Pass out copies of "When We Say *All*, Do We Mean All?" and read aloud the "Eat a Good Breakfast" vignette.

2. Tell the group how easy it is to fall back on assumptions such as the mistake made in the vignette where the principal reminded all students to "eat a good breakfast."

3. Have participants review each school activity in "When We Say *All*, Do We Mean All?" and discuss whether each includes all students and families. Follow the prompts above each column in "When We Say *All*, Do We Mean All?"

4. After the groups have completed the columns task, discuss, as a whole group, which activities the majority of the group found inclusive and which the majority did not find inclusive. Then discuss what impact that has on students, families, and the staff's relationships with caregivers.

5. Call on diverse caregivers (such as parents, grandparents, and other guardians) from various backgrounds to perform the same audit and discussion. Which activities do they consider exclusionary, and what could help include them? Allow for and request their voices and listen to their suggestions. When appropriate, implement their suggestions. This reinforces the important role they play as partners with the school. Find a way to thank them for their contribution and then enact what changes they have suggested that you can make.

6. Ensure that the suggested changes to promote inclusivity and the impact of these new activities or initiatives are addressed each semester, with staff and stakeholder opinions at the fore. Your school may have a campus improvement plan, reviewed at least three times a year, that is considered a road map for the school's direction and goals. A scheduled review is an excellent time to discuss how well the initiatives on compassion and inclusivity are being addressed.

Directions for independent practice follow.

1. Make a copy of "When We Say *All*, Do We Mean All?" and read the "Eat a Good Breakfast" vignette.

2. Remember how easy it is to fall back on assumptions such as the mistake made in the vignette where the principal reminded all students to "eat a good breakfast."

3. Look at each school activity and decide if it is inclusive. Follow the prompts above each column on "When We Say *All*, Do We Mean All?"

4. Are most activities inclusive? Those that are inclusive, how do they manage that? Those that are not, how could they change? What impact does this have on students? The takeaway here is in recognizing the need to remove barriers that may inadvertently sideline groups of people, causing them to feel marginalized.

Life Situations

Open our hearts and minds to the fact that life circumstances can be vastly different from one family to another. A myriad of factors determines why someone makes a decision. It takes stepping away from our own perspective and considering someone else's to begin the process of practicing deeper empathy and understanding and accepting others.

Objective: To make decisions from another person's perspective after placing ourselves in different life situations and to learn not to judge without knowing another person's story.

Materials: 4 × 6" cardstock paper (enough to print one set of Life Situation Cards per group of four or five people), 5 × 7" envelopes (one per group of four or five people), chart paper, markers, journal or paper, "The Tennis Shoes" vignette (page 42), and reproducible "Life Situation Cards" (page 64)

Directions for facilitated group practice follow.

1. Prior to the meeting, copy the six Life Situation Cards onto cardstock. Depending on the number of groups, you may need multiple copies of each. Consider customizing cards specific to your campus.

2. Cut out the cards individually.

3. Place each card in a 5 × 7" envelope.

4. Write the corresponding life situation number scenario on the front of each envelope (*one*, *two*, *three*, and so on).

5. During the meeting, read aloud "The Tennis Shoes" vignette from the start of this chapter.

6. Break into groups of four or five.

7. Explain that you will be passing out an envelope to each group. Groups are not to open these envelopes until the objectives have been discussed.

8. Explain that these situations have been derived closely from real-life situations. No names will ever be used, and some of the details may have been changed to protect identities.

9. Randomly pass out the labeled 5 × 7" envelopes.

10. Announce that groups have fifteen or twenty minutes to read their Life Situation Card, come to a consensus on what to do complete with steps, and provide a rationale for the decision. On chart paper, they list their decisions and the steps they would take. At the bottom of the chart paper, they write the rationale.

11. Each small group shares with the whole group, focusing on understanding how unfair it is to make judgments about a person or situation one does not understand.

Directions for independent practice follow.

1. Read "The Tennis Shoes" vignette from the start of this chapter.

2. Look over the "Life Situation Cards" and choose one. These situations derive from real life.

3. Come up with a plan of what to do and the rationale for your decisions. On either a piece of paper or a large piece of chart paper, write a list of your decisions and the steps you took. At the bottom of the paper, write why you made that decision.

4. Ask yourself the following questions.

    • "Do I feel comfortable with the decision I made?"

    • "What was the most difficult part of making this decision?"

    • "If I were in this same position, where could I go for help?"

5. Would you be able to justify your choices when there are few to no good options? The takeaway is that sometimes, life's choices are limited.

Try It in the Classroom

The Life Situations activity (page 49) can easily be adapted for teaching students in the classroom. Create age-appropriate scenarios on cards for children about making choices to act with kindness and compassion, with the questions after each scenario being, "What would you do?" and "What is the kind and compassionate action to take?" Either discuss the card scenarios as a whole class or divide the class into small groups to discuss. Read the following example and ask yourself what you would do and what compassionate action should be taken.

You see a student eating lunch alone every day. This student may look a little different in appearance than most of the students on the campus. You have noticed when other students look at them, they quickly avoid eye contact. At times, you have seen other students snicker at them as they walk by.

Walking in My Shoes

This activity demonstrates that people are more alike than different.

Objective: To identify life experiences that all humanity has in common, and to create connections with others through the practice of thoughtful listening and acknowledging our likenesses rather than our differences.

Materials: Reproducibles "More Alike Than Different" (page 67) and "Walk in My Shoes" (page 68), scissors, card stock (for printing the latter reproducible), one large sheet of chart paper, two containers (baskets or something similar) with one labeled *group A* and the other labeled *group B*, and writing utensils

Directions for facilitated group practice follow.

1. To prepare, print the two pages of the "Walk in My Shoes" reproducible front to back and cut on the dotted line so each card is a half sheet.

2. Ask participants to look around the room. Remind them that all lives look different. We may look different, be from different places, and have different experiences, but we have things in common.

3. Give each participant a copy of "More Alike Than Different" to read. Explain that this activity demonstrates that, although we may appear unique, a common strand of humanity runs through us and our lives. Shoes, like people, are varied. Are you young and sporty with a spring

in your step, or are you sure-footed and tough? Are you risky and wanting to dazzle, or tired and needing comfort? Are you climbing the ladder in your career or slowing down in age? What's your story?

4. Request a volunteer to scribe on chart paper. Ask for a few volunteers or groups to come up with more statements about commonalities that are not on the list. The scribe records these so they are visible to the group.

5. Divide into two groups, A and B. There should be an equal number of participants on both teams. If one group is short a person, the presenter joins that group. If your group is large, break into groups of ten or twelve.

6. Pass out a copy of "Walk in My Shoes" to each participant.

7. Have participants write their name and assigned group letter (such as *Susan S., group A*) on the side of the card that has footwear and then circle the picture of the footwear they feel best fits their life. Participants should respond to the questions on the other side of the cards aloud to their partners.

8. Ask group A to fold their cards with pictures of the shoes on the inside and place them in the group A basket. Ask group B to fold their cards with pictures of the shoes on the inside and place their cards in the group B basket.

9. Without looking at the sheets, each person in group A chooses a card from group B's basket.

10. Partner A pairs up with the person whose card he, she, or they chose from group B. Partner A listens to partner B's response to the questions on the back of the card.

11. Provide enough time for talking to subside. Remind participants to thank each other for sharing. When talking subsides, explain to the group that thanking our work partners is a great strategy to use in the classroom. When students are working in pairs or groups, the kind thing for them to do is thank their partners.

12. Ask participants to switch roles. Again, without looking, group B participants choose a card from group A's basket.

13. Partner B pairs up with the person whose card he, she, or they chose from group A. Partner B listens to partner A's responses to the same questions on the back of the card.

14. Remind participants that although sharing about ourselves may sometimes feel awkward, vulnerable, or even emotional, this is how human connections are formed. We share and learn about each other. Walking through an activity like this, which might be duplicated in the classroom, provides educators an opportunity to internalize the experience before walking students through it.

Directions for independent practice follow.

1. Make two copies of "Walk in My Shoes" and have one blank piece of paper available.

2. Read "More Alike Than Different."

3. Write a few more statements that you think are missing from the list.

4. On "Walk in My Shoes," circle the footwear that best fits your life.

5. On the other side of your card, write your answers to the questions that appear there.

6. For your second card, think of someone you work with daily or someone in your circle of friends. Write that person's name on the inside of the card.

7. Circle the footwear on the front of the card you believe that person would choose.

8. Answer the same two questions from what you believe would be their point of view, so you do some perspective-taking (Abramson, 2021).

9. For your own reflection, use the blank piece of paper to answer the following questions.

   • How different or alike are the responses from your own card versus the second card?

   • What challenges did you have in completing the card from someone else's viewpoint?

10. Consider sharing the second card you created with the person you chose. Ask that person if the responses would have been similar or quite different.

Try It in the Classroom

Walking in My Shoes (page 51) is an appropriate activity for most upper-elementary and secondary students. This activity helps students get to know each other better and works anytime during the school year. Introduce the activity with a class discussion on what human experiences students of their age share. Remind students that walking through these common experiences may look different for each person.

Judge Softly

This activity provides a quiet time of reflection as participants listen to a poem being read aloud. While the poem may ask you to put yourself in someone else's shoes, "How you take the perspective can make a difference," since imagining yourself "in another person's position" may lead to "a lot of personal distress, which can interfere with prosocial behavior" (Dovidio, as cited in Abramson, 2021). This activity is not the same thing. We are not diving deeply into the issues of others—only attempting to understand their perspective. However, when asked to practice empathy, remember that it is not the kind that requires you to consistently place yourself in another person's shoes.

Objective: To listen to words written over 125 years ago and identify how these words still ring true today. Humans continue to strive for understanding others through empathy and compassion.

Materials: Reproducible "Judge Softly" (page 70) and document camera, computer with projection screen, or whiteboard

Directions for facilitated group and independent practice follow.

1. Read aloud the stanzas from the poem "Judge Softly" by Mary T. Lathrap (1895) to participants. Read slowly and with emphasis. For our purpose, some stanzas have been omitted.

2. Display the following questions so participants can read them. Let them know they have three minutes for silent reflection.

   - What difficult decision have you faced in your life?

   - What made the decision difficult? Did someone walk softly with you to make the experience easier?

   - Did you show yourself compassion?

3. At the end of the three minutes, reread the stanzas one more time. Mention that over 125 years later, the words still ring true.

4. Ask the participants to sit in silence for two minutes and think on the following lines: "We will be known forever by the tracks we leave in other people's lives, our kindnesses and generosity" (Lathrap, 1895).

5. At the end of the two minutes of silence, quietly ask participants, "As a human being, and more specifically as an educator, how will you leave behind tracks of kindness and generosity?" The question is for self-reflection. Sit in silence with the question for at least five seconds before either ending the day's lesson or continuing on to another activity.

Unexpected Conversations

In the constraints of an educator's world, one that is dictated by rigid schedules and bells, it isn't often we have time to simply share our thoughts and reflect on deep conversations with our colleagues. We can learn much from exchanging ideas and gaining insights through other peoples' perspectives.

Objective: To share personal perspectives through individual responses to guided questions.

Materials: One die per group and the reproducibles "Eat a Good Breakfast" (page 62) and "Unexpected Conversations" (page 71)

Directions for facilitated group practice follow.

1. Share the "Eat a Good Breakfast" vignette.

2. Before handing out materials, remind everyone to be honest and reflective. This is an opportunity for everyone to be heard, and there are no wrong answers.

3. Break into groups of four or five.

4. Provide one die to each group and give each person one copy of "Unexpected Conversations."

5. The person in each group whose last name has the most letters begins the activity. If there is a tie, the person who rolls the highest number on the die goes first. The group members take turns.

6. Call time after you feel the groups have had the chance to circle through two or three times.

7. Ask participants to thank their group members for sharing. Mention this is another opportunity to practice kindness. It is what we want to model for students in the classroom.

The takeaway from this activity is that teaching is as much an emotional job as it is an academic job. We learn from our experiences, both positive and negative. Educators are in the process of constantly learning and adjusting.

Directions for independent practice follow.

1. Read the "Eat a Good Breakfast" reproducible.

2. Have a copy of "Unexpected Conversations" and one die.

3. Roll the die to answer the prompts at random or answer all the prompts. Be honest and reflective with your answers.

4. Ask yourself whether, if you were to answer these prompts in front of colleagues, your answers would be the same. If your answer is *no*, why would you feel the need to change your answers?

Tip

We all have a circle of influence—a large net we cast on the people we touch with our words and actions. Every one of us, in whatever roles we have at work or home, can positively impact people with compassion. The words we speak and the decisions we make influence our families, colleagues, students, and communities. Model the message you want others to receive.

Administrators: In your circle of influence, how can you model the message of caring, compassion, and inclusion for your faculty and staff? Look for small changes that send a positive message, such as including teachers in decision making, honoring planning and conference times, being accessible, ensuring supplies are easily available, visiting classrooms, providing treats in the faculty lounge, checking in with a phone call if a teacher is out due to surgery or a death in the family, recognizing faculty and staff for doing something special or simply for showing the compassion your campus seeks to show each other.

Teacher voice is a big part of employee satisfaction in schools, so asking for a teacher's opinion and honoring it when you can goes a long way toward creating the kind of compassionate culture you seek and the kinds of relationships that you want with staff:

> Research shows that when teachers are engaged in school decisions and collaborate with administrators and each other, school climate improves. This

promotes a better learning environment for students, which raises student achievement, and a better working environment for teachers, which reduces teacher turnover. (Kahlenberg & Potter, 2014)

I once visited a campus where all the teacher supplies were kept behind locked cabinet doors. The only person with a key was the school secretary. If a teacher needed something, they had to ask the secretary, who would then unlock the cabinet and count out the number of pencils, sheets of paper, or paper clips needed. What message does this send?

Teachers: In your circle of influence, how can you model the message of caring, compassion, and inclusion for your students? Look for small changes that will send a positive message, such as intentional seating arrangements, free access to needed supplies, private communication (such as a class mailbox with blank index cards nearby), discussing meaningful quotes from texts you're reading, having class conversations where everyone's voice is respected, apologizing if you mess up, noticing students' interests, and recognizing when a student shows compassion.

Listen when students want to share. Hearing their voices matters, since "students who believe they have a voice in school are seven times more likely to be academically motivated . . . [which can lead] to an increased likelihood that students will experience self-worth, engagement, and purpose in school" (St. John & Briel, 2017, p. 1).

Listen With Your Eyes

Communication is more than just words. We use facial expressions and body language to say more than we realize. Because a person cannot speak it does not mean they cannot communicate. This activity is a lesson in communicating without words. Students can walk into a classroom with a teacher standing at the classroom door with arms folded and eyes elsewhere, or their teacher can be smiling at them, waving. Teachers determine what type of image they want to project. Just like adults, students have good and bad days. If you greet students in a welcoming way at the door, you have a much better chance of gauging who needs a little more compassion that day. If you notice a student seeming sad, angry, or frustrated, jot a quick, *Are you OK?* on a sticky note and inconspicuously pass it to them. Your compassion will speak volumes.

As a presenter, you may decide to have participants do this Are You OK? strategy independently and at a later date have them share their experiences.

Objective: To use only nonverbal communication and form a single line of people in the order of the month and day of their birthdays.

Materials: A whistle and a space large enough for all participants to line up; for independent practice, reproducible "Nonverbal Communication" (page 72)

Directions for facilitated group practice follow.

1. Remind participants that we use nonverbal facial expressions or body language to express ourselves.

2. Tell participants they will be forming a line in order of their birthday month and day without using any words.

3. Explain to participants that this activity's success looks, sounds, and feels like the following.

    - *Looks like* all participants walking around the room communicating their birthdays to determine where their place is in line.

    - *Sounds like* silence.

    - *Feels like* cooperation and patience.

4. When you sound the whistle's signal, the activity begins.

5. When the group feels it has completed the task successfully, participants raise their hands.

6. Check that the participants have lined themselves up correctly. Without speaking, find the end of the line that represents January. Walk down the line as each participant, using nonverbal communication, indicates their birth month and date.

7. If someone has lined up incorrectly, the participant is provided the chance to fix the situation.

8. Once you confirm everyone is in their correct spot, sound the whistle that talking may resume.

9. Post the following questions for verbal communication after everyone takes a seat.

    - Did you find this activity easier or more difficult than you expected? Why?

    - What emotions did you feel?

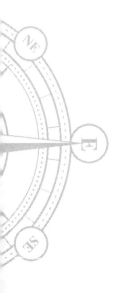

10. Remind participants that they have discovered that they do not need words to send messages. They can use body language intentionally to signal acceptance and compassion.

You can conduct this activity as a competition. Randomly divide the group in half. Tell both teams that when you sound the signal, there is no more talking. Again, the goal is to line up by birth month and day. The team that correctly completes the challenge first is the winner. You may want inexpensive prizes for those on the winning team.

Try It in the Classroom

Students love this activity. Ask them to pay attention and listen with their eyes. They will be looking for facial expressions and body language. Participation demonstrates that words aren't always necessary to communicate.

Directions for independent practice follow.

1. Commit to a day and time (about an hour) to observe random peoples' facial expressions and body language. Using the "Nonverbal Communication" reproducible, keep a tally of the number of times you see what a person is communicating (without hearing their conversations) by observing their facial expressions and body language.

2. After tallying, consider the following questions.

   - What emotions were most easily identifiable?

   - What communication was hardest to identify?

   - Do you think that the time of day of your observations made a difference in your observations?

3. Reflect on the following questions.

   - Are there times you try to hide how you feel?

   - If so, how successful do you think you are at hiding your nonverbal communication?

4. Remind yourself to be aware of how easy it is to interpret a person's body language. People speak loudly and clearly if you listen and watch.

You can perform this activity by watching television without the sound on.

Next Steps

If you see a colleague having a bad day, take a small step. Take them a snack or a bottle of water, place a note on their desk, or ask if they'd like to talk during lunch or take a walk around the campus after school. Ask directly if and how you can help. The same goes for students. Place a note on their desk, invite them and a friend to have lunch with you, ask if they have an adult they can talk to, or offer to listen. It's the little moments that say, "I see you" that count.

Our work and school environments allow us to engage with people from all walks of life who may be different from our own. In strengthening these relationships, we are afforded the opportunity to view another person's perspective.

Common Questions

Two common questions around acceptance are (1) How can we encourage students to be less judgmental? and (2) What opportunity can be provided to learn acceptance and inclusion outside of the classroom?

How Can We Encourage Students to Be Less Judgmental?

Provide students with the opportunity to work alongside people who are different from them (Gino & Coffman, 2021). You can accomplish this in different ways.

- **Mindfully assign seats and intentionally assign project partners:** Keep in mind skill levels, personalities, and social power when creating pairs or groups. Working in small groups benefits not only the new students but all students in the class by potentially helping them "develop social and leadership skills" and may "draw people out who normally would not participate in front of the whole class. It also promotes self-esteem as compared to competitive or individualistic learning" (Harvard Kennedy School, n.d.).

- **Pair up with a class of students who have special needs:** Work with the principal and the other teacher to organize special days, activities, and opportunities to blend classes. Planning and preparations (for both teachers and students) need to take place before these opportunities occur. Check out www.bestbuddies.org /what-we-do/friendship if you don't have a Best Buddies chapter at your middle or high school; it is a volunteer organization that pairs one member who has an intellectual or developmental disability with a peer who does not.

What Opportunity Can Be Provided to Learn Acceptance and Inclusion Outside the Classroom?

One of the best ideas I have come across is having a class or club adopt a nearby nursing home and visit on regularly scheduled dates. The elderly are an often-overlooked population for opportunities for inclusion and acceptance. Make arrangements for a scheduled visit. Ask about the parameters of what students can and cannot do during a visit. If possible, have a representative from the nursing home come and speak with the class so students understand what to expect. A few examples of things to do during a visit follow.

- Take a resident on a stroll in their wheelchair.

- Take a walk outside with a resident (if permitted) to get some fresh air.

- Play board games (like checkers or chess) or card games.

- Help them write letters if they no longer can hold a pen.

- Simply have a conversation with them.

If students are unsure what to talk with the residents about, suggest they ask the residents about their lives. Most have interesting stories to share.

Reflection Questions

Consider the following questions, perhaps with a colleague.

- Has a student ever confided in you about something personal? How did you respond?

- What things have you done (or what can you do) to earn the trust of your students' caregivers?

- Would all your students be able to agree that you are inclusive in your classroom?

- Would your students (or colleagues) be able to name ways that demonstrate you know them as individuals and not simply as a collective group?

- Is there a person or a group you have not seen or acknowledged?

Eat a Good Breakfast

"I've thought of everything!" she thought.

As a novice principal, Erica Henderson was nervous about being fully prepared for the imminent standardized testing. Because she knew how much importance her district placed on the results, she found herself waking in the middle of the night writing notes about the testing schedule, the placement of classrooms, the personnel who would monitor, and ensuring coverage for teachers to provide bathroom breaks. She was determined to address every schedule, every monitor, and every possible scenario.

She had seen how hard the teachers and students had been working. Staff held meetings to evaluate student progress, ordered materials, and provided after-school tutoring; teams reviewed lesson plans; students took practice tests; and teachers (with students) and administrators (with teachers) discussed expectations—repeatedly.

With tests slated to start the following day and the dismissal bell about to ring, Erica turned on the intercom system to make the day's final announcement: "As you know, tomorrow is an important day. Your teachers have prepared you well, and you have worked hard to be ready for the test. However, get to bed early tonight and eat a good breakfast in the morning. These things will help you do your best. We believe in you!"

Erica leaned back in her chair when she heard a whisper of a voice say, "Ms. Henderson?" Clarissa, a small, quiet fourth grader, poked her head through the open door to the office.

"What's up, Clarissa?"

"You know how you said in the announcement that to do our best we need to go to bed early and eat a good breakfast?" Clarissa was hesitant, and Erica nodded to encourage her to go on.

"Well, I really do want to do my best, but we won't have much food at our house until Friday. My mom gets paid on Friday."

Erica questioned herself: How could she have not thought about the implications of that announcement? How many times did she and the staff talk about the challenges so many of their students face?

"Clarissa, thank you for letting me know. Let me see what we can do."

At the after-school faculty meeting that day, Erica took a deep breath and said, "I need to apologize for my lack of thinking. I told the students who are being tested tomorrow to go to bed early and eat a good breakfast. Many of our kids may not be able to do those things. I apologize for not being more thoughtful."

Afterward, Erica and the school's family specialist delivered a few groceries to Clarissa's home—but she couldn't deliver groceries to all the students who may have needed food.

When We Say *All*, Do We Mean All?

School Event	Barriers Preventing All Students From Participating Examples: money, transportation, lack of personal connection, social cliques on campus, family problems, physical or cognitive limitations, having English as a second language	How the Event Could Be More Inclusive
Festival		
Grandparents' day		
Career day		
Pep rally or spirit day		
Book fair		
Picture day		
Field trip		
Visiting author days		
Game day		
Campus clubs		
Other:		
Other:		

Life Situation Cards

Life Situation One

Your two children (ages four and seven) are sick with bad colds and coughs. You recently lost your job from multiple absences due to staying at home with your children when they were ill.

Due to a lack of money, you have no medicine for the children. The refrigerator is empty. There is no heat because the electricity has been turned off. You have been unable to look for work because you are new in town and cannot leave the children unattended.

You just received a letter from the school district that your children have excessive absences and that you may have to go to court because of it.

What would you do? Explain your reasoning.

Life Situation Two

Your middle child was nominated to attend a free summer camp. To ensure your child is saved a spot at the camp, a parent must attend a meeting. There are no exceptions. The award ceremony is at 10:00 a.m. tomorrow. The teacher wrote you a note saying how important it would be for your child to have this all-expenses-paid, once-in-a-lifetime experience.

Your car battery is dead, and you have no money to buy a new one. You have been getting to work (which is forty-five minutes across town) by bus and making two bus changes every trip. You cannot afford to miss work.

What would you do? Explain your reasoning.

Life Situation Three

You have a six-year-old child and have stayed home raising her. All your immediate family lives in another country.

You do not associate with your neighbors because you have not learned their language, and you are not a registered citizen. For this same reason, you have rarely stepped foot into the school your child attends.

Your spouse drives a truck for a living, and that is your sole income. It is just enough to cover the bills. There is no money in savings. You do not own a vehicle.

You just found out your husband has been killed in a truck accident.

What would you do? Explain your reasoning.

Life Situation Four

Due to a natural disaster, you and your children were evacuated and relocated to another city for an unknown period. All you have in your pocket is $45.

Your three children have been in their new schools for about three weeks. They are angry and frustrated. Teachers are sending notes home requesting conferences because your children are acting out.

Your family is being allowed to live in a small hotel room in exchange for cleaning rooms during the day; there is no other pay for the work. If you miss a day of cleaning, your family must sleep in the car. You have been unsuccessfully looking for a job.

You need money for a deposit on an apartment and utilities.

What would you do? Explain your reasoning.

Life Situation Five

You are a recovering drug addict. You have worked hard toward your recovery and are now caring for your children, who had to spend time away in foster care. Smoking cigarettes is the one vice that calms your anxiety, and it helps you stay drug free.

You and your children live with your grandmother in a one-bedroom apartment. You don't pay rent, but you help your grandmother buy groceries and medication.

You are experiencing major anxiety about the possibility of losing your minimum-wage job due to personnel cuts. You are out of cigarettes. It is twelve days until payday. With your last $13, which one of the following do you buy?

- Your grandmother's heart medication
- Beans, hot dogs, bread, and peanut butter for the family to eat
- A pack of cigarettes to help you get through the stress without using drugs
- Diapers for the baby
- A bus pass to get to work

What would you do? Explain your reasoning.

Compassion as Our Compass © 2024 Solution Tree Press • SolutionTree.com
Visit **go.SolutionTree.com/teacherefficacy** to download this free reproducible.

Life Situation Six

You grew up in and out of homeless shelters with your mother and sibling. At fifteen, you dropped out of high school to earn money for the household.

You now have a daughter of your own, who is six years old. She has never attended school. It is October. Both of you have been living out of an abandoned bus for a year.

When you try to register your daughter for school, you do not have the necessary paperwork—birth certificate, vaccination records, or permanent address verification.

You have confided to the school counselor that you recently found out you have cancer.

What would you do? Explain your reasoning.

More Alike Than Different

All our stories are connected by the thread of humanity. Examples of such stories and connections follow.

- Life milestones

- People we love

- Pets who are part of our family

- Hobbies we enjoy

- Goals we want to accomplish

- Children, grandchildren, great-grandchildren, or elders we provide care for

- Weddings to anticipate, attend, or plan

- Babies to welcome into the family

- Illness of a loved one

- The empty nest

- Just starting a new job

- A new relationship or the ending of one

- Distant relatives we'd love to see

- Places we hope to visit

- Anniversaries of occasions both happy and sad

- Worries that keep us up at night

- Books we are reading and movies and shows we're watching

- Planning for the future—for ourselves or our children

- Celebrations, traditions, or rites of passage

Walk in My Shoes

Circle the picture of the shoe that best fits your life.

- -

Circle the picture of the shoe that best fits your life.

page 1 of 2

Why did you choose the footwear you circled? If I walk in your shoes today, what would life look like to me?

- -

Why did you choose the footwear you circled? If I walk in your shoes today, what would life look like to me?

Judge Softly

By Mary T. Lathrap

Pray, don't find fault with the man that limps,

Or stumbles along the road.

Unless you have worn the moccasins he wears,

Or stumbled beneath the same load.

There may be tears in his soles that hurt

Though hidden away from view.

The burden he bears placed on your back

May cause you to stumble and fall, too.

Don't sneer at the man who is down today

Unless you have felt the same blow

That caused his fall or felt the shame

That only the fallen know.

. . .

Just walk a mile in his moccasins

Before you abuse, criticize and accuse.

If just for one hour, you could find a way

To see through his eyes, instead of your own muse.

I believe you'd be surprised to see

That you've been blind and narrow minded, even unkind.

. . .

We will be known forever by the tracks we leave in other people's lives,

our kindnesses and generosity.

Take the time to walk a mile in his moccasins.

Source

Lathrap, M. T. (1895). *Rare gems from the literary works of Mary T. Lathrap: Born April 25, 1838, died January 3, 1895.* Cleveland, OH: Woman's Christian Temperance Union.

Unexpected Conversations

In your group, take turns rolling one die and answer the corresponding prompts. If you roll a number you have already answered, roll again. Repeat until time is called. Respect everyone's opinions and ideas. There are no wrong answers.

Share an interaction you had with a student that you would change if you had the chance at a do-over. 1	We are always learning lessons. What is a big life lesson (personal or professional) you have learned over the past three years? 2	At times, life creates hard choices. These choices may involve choosing between food, shelter, or medicine. If you had to choose only one, which do you feel would be the most important? Explain your choice. 3
Name a specific person you feel you have inspired and describe how you had an impact on them. 4	Has there been a time you said something to a student or caregiver but the message was misunderstood? Explain. 5	What is something you need consistently to inspire your passion for your work? How can you achieve this? 6

Nonverbal Communication

Day:

Time:

Expressions to Look For (Without Having Heard a Conversation)	Tally	Notes
Anger		
Apathy		
Excitement		
Fear		
Frustration		
Happiness		
Hopelessness		
Inquisitiveness		
Loneliness		
Love		
Sadness		
Other:		

CHAPTER 4
Understanding Our Roles

I cannot be a teacher without exposing who I am.

— PAULO FREIRE

Educators wear many hats: teacher, social worker, counselor, friend, mentor, organizer, researcher, curriculum specialist, planner, consoler, cheerleader, and investigator are just a few. All these roles help educators make informed decisions about what to provide students, whose needs vary dramatically. Teachers are caregivers, and most caregivers are compassionate and empathic. The roles of supporter, cheerleader, motivator, counselor, social worker, investigator, and friend are all tied up in the work of being an educator. Wanting to help, support, and encourage students is our calling.

As in the following vignette, purposeful plans with the best intentions may be implemented, but are there times when plans backfire? Yes. When someone is under severe stress:

> The carefully orchestrated yet near-instantaneous sequence of hormonal changes and physiological responses helps someone to fight the threat off or flee to safety. Unfortunately, the body can also overreact to stressors that are not life-threatening, such as traffic jams, work pressure, and family difficulties. (Harvard Health, 2020)

The following vignette demonstrates that the role of an educator is not a nine-to-five job. The responsibilities don't stop when you leave the campus. Educators carry the emotional weight and responsibilities. This outcome was not what was expected. But we persevere.

Five-Thirty in the Morning

At 5:30 a.m., elementary school principal Dr. Erika Jess turns on the tiny, metal flashlight attached to her car keys. As she walks up the elementary school steps, the flashlight shines on a small human figure. Dr. Jess is startled, but it takes just a couple of seconds to realize the figure is a small boy sitting alone.

"Oh, my gosh! You scared me! What are you doing here so early?" Dr. Jess says aloud.

"My dad dropped me off."

"Why so early?"

"He has to go to work."

"Do you sit here every morning by yourself?"

"Yes."

After learning the student is named Kenneth, bringing him in, and providing a snack and some water for him, Dr. Jess looks up Kenneth's contact information. There is no working home number, so she calls the work number listed on the card. The person who answers is obviously irritated and says Kenneth's father is working and can't come to the phone. Dr. Jess leaves a message for his dad to call her back.

Dr. Jess shares what she knows with Ms. Trevino (Kenneth's teacher) and Mr. Grayson (the school counselor), and they file a report with child protective services. Leaving a six-year-old child outside alone at 5:30 a.m. is child endangerment or neglect. By the end of the day, Dr. Jess still hasn't heard back from Kenneth's dad.

Dr. Jess figures they can speak with Kenneth's dad at school the next morning at 5:15 a.m. Sitting in the dimly lit school parking lot with Ms. Trevino, Dr. Jess begins to question the decision.

When a car pulls up and Kenneth gets out of it, Dr. Jess and Ms. Trevino say a loud greeting to avoid frightening them as they approach the car.

"You'll need to find other arrangements," explains Dr. Jess. "We don't have staff to watch students at 5:30 a.m."

"I can't miss work," Kenneth's dad responds.

"Can a neighbor watch him?" asks Ms. Trevino.

"I don't know any neighbors."

"Sir, it is not safe for Kenneth to be at school at 5:30 in the morning. Can we—" Before Dr. Jess finishes, Kenneth's dad abruptly drives out of the parking lot.

Dr. Jess and Ms. Trevino share what happened with the counselor, Mr. Grayson. The three agree to visit Kenneth's apartment after school when his dad is normally home. The group knocks several times, but there is no answer at the door.

Kenneth is absent from school the following morning. The next day and the following day, there's still no Kenneth and no return phone calls from his father. After three days of calling his work number, the man's employer answers and says, "He no longer works here. He told us he had to move where the school would stay out of his business."

Kenneth never returns to that school.

Can it be that when trying to do the right thing, the wrong thing can happen? Yes, but we continue to make decisions in the best interest of our students, even when we don't know for certain what the outcome will be. At times we make emotional decisions based on whatever hat we are wearing at the time, be it teacher, mentor, cheerleader, counselor, or friend. When Dr. Jess approached the car, she was wearing multiple hats of teacher, counselor, and social worker. Compassion had moved Dr. Jess to step outside the classroom walls and outside the normal school day to ensure the safety and well-being of a student. This is the heart of a caring educator.

Why We Need to Understand Our Multiple Roles

It is important to understand that meeting the needs of students is not solely academic. This is where an educator's ability to play multiple roles comes in. We try to reach the whole child. You could use the term *social accountability*, which is "that most natural and essential check on human behavior" (Malone & Fiske, 2013, p. 14), to describe what educators do daily. We set the stage and create conditions that promote learning to take place. Over the course of a day, educators may show compassion in a dozen different ways, from listening to a student who needs to be heard, to nursing a student with a skinned knee, to cheering on the student who has much self-doubt, to mentoring the young person who just became a co-worker, fresh out of school. We care for our students emotionally, physically, and socially, as well as academically.

Because the demands on educators are multilayered, we tend to carry the weight of our own and others' emotional baggage. Carrying this extra weight and ignoring the toll can lead to teacher burnout, which is "chronic workplace stress . . . characterized by three dimensions: (1) feelings of energy depletion or exhaustion; (2) increased mental distance from one's job, or feelings of negativism or cynicism related to one's job; and (3) reduced professional efficacy" (World Health Organization, 2019). This fact, and its prevalence, make it important for educators to care for themselves. Burnout affects a person's quality of life and mental and physical health, and it does not just affect teachers: "Student performance can be adversely affected by teacher stress" (Bouchrika, 2023). It is difficult to be inspired by a teacher who lacks joy or motivation, and it is difficult, if not impossible, to show compassion when we are depleted.

Here are some lessons learned.

- **Keep yourself out of harm's way as much as possible:** We cannot know a parent's emotional state. If phone calls or a home visit (or two) don't result in being able to speak reasonably with a parent, use the support of your campus or district personnel.

- **Continue to persevere even when setbacks occur:** Success comes from not giving up. Though, again, it's important to care for yourself, set boundaries, ask for help, dig in, and show grit. In this case, think of grit as "awareness and self-management" (Lan, 2022). When struggling to stick with something during an unexpected or particularly difficult challenge, for example, co-workers can be great sounding boards and encouragers. They are familiar with the demands of the job and can, ideally, empathize.

Activities for Understanding Our Roles

The following are activities for understanding the many hats that educators wear on a daily basis. These activities are reminders that educators slide between or straddle roles as needed daily. Teachers in a room of students do not only teach curricula. The classroom presents abundant opportunities to model compassion and acceptance. The care, guidance, modeling, encouragement, and support teachers provide comes from wearing all kinds of hats and this work is immeasurable.

Mindful and Meaningful Roles

This strategy provides educators the opportunity to share what roles they played in making a difference in the life of a student or a student's family.

Objective: To identify the varied roles of educators and the importance of each role.

Materials: One small bag of multicolored candy per participant, chart paper, markers, "Five-Thirty in the Morning" vignette (page 74), and the reproducible "Mindful and Meaningful Roles" (page 85)

Directions for facilitated group practice follow.

1. Share the "Five-Thirty in the Morning" vignette.

2. Break into groups of four to six.

3. Ask each group to write a list of roles educators play on the chart paper.

4. Pass out one bag of multicolored candy and one copy of "Mindful and Meaningful Roles" to each participant.

5. In a clockwise direction, the first participant pulls one piece of candy from the bag and responds to the question that corresponds to the candy's color.

   - *Green:* Which role do you play most often? Why?

   - *Blue or purple:* When is a time you could have done more for someone, whether a student, family, or friend, by playing a different role? What more could you have done?

   - *Yellow:* What role are you best at performing? Why?

   - *Red:* What is the hardest decision you have had to make as an educator?

   - *Orange:* What role do you find the most difficult? Why?

   - *Brown:* What is something you wish a teacher had done for you when you were a student? Have you had the opportunity to do something similar for a student? Explain.

6. Take turns, going clockwise around the circle at least twice. If participants get stuck, they may ask for help from someone in their group or ask for help from someone in another group.

7. After all groups have had the opportunity to provide each person with two opportunities to share, ask the groups to create their own definition of *educator* and have them write it at the bottom of their chart.

8. Compare the definitions of each group by asking for volunteers to read their definitions out loud. Ask the group to recognize that their role as a teacher is so much more than teaching curricula.

Directions for independent practice follow.

1. Read the "Five-Thirty in the Morning" vignette.

2. Think of all the roles you feel educators play and write them on a piece of paper.

3. Open the bag of multicolored candy, take out one piece, and respond to the question on "Mindful and Meaningful Roles" that corresponds to the color you picked.

4. Repeat that step at least three times. If you repeatedly pull out the same color, eat them (or move them aside) until you get a new color.

5. Write your own definition of *educator* at the bottom of the same paper where you listed educator roles.

6. Remembering a time that you'd like a do-over may cause you to pause and wince. How could reflecting on these events impact your decisions or actions in the future?

Try It in the Classroom

Students love participating in an activity that uses candy. You can revise the questions on "Mindful and Meaningful Roles" (page 85) to make them age appropriate. Follow the facilitated group practice directions. The questions can center on compassion, but this strategy can also work to review a specific topic or text. Examples for using Mindful and Meaningful Roles in the classroom follow.

This is an *elementary* example of a friends unit. Remind students *not* to use names of people when they respond to the questions.

- **Green:** Do you feel you are a good friend? Why?

- **Blue or purple:** What could you do for someone today that would show friendship?

- **Yellow:** In your own words, describe what the word *friend* means.

- **Red:** What is the nicest thing you have done for a friend or relative?

- **Orange:** Is it ever hard to be friends with someone? Why was it hard?

- **Brown:** What is the nicest thing a friend has ever done for you?

This is a *secondary* example with questions about U.S. history.

- **Green:** What roles did George Washington play in the forming of the country?

- **Blue or purple:** The country was split between the Loyalists and the Patriots. Pick a side and describe why that side felt the way it did.

- **Yellow:** Explain how Paul Revere warned the colonists the British were coming.

- **Red:** Families and friends sometimes supported different sides. If you were a Patriot and your favorite cousin was a Loyalist to Great Britain, how would you feel if you spotted each fighting on different sides of the battlefield? How do you think you would react?

- **Orange:** What do you feel gave the Patriots the determination to continue in combat when they were low on food and without proper clothing?

- **Brown:** In what ways, at that time in history, could women support the soldiers?

For both the elementary and secondary levels, you can use any story to create questions about the viewpoints of the main characters. In social studies, ask questions about the time, place, culture, and events that took place being studied. For mathematics and science, ask discovery questions (*why*) during or after experiments.

Comment and Clip It

The strength of trusting everyone's input is demonstrated during Comment and Clip It. As participants go through this activity in small groups, each person in the group has the responsibility for one piece of the total group response. Individual responses remain secret until the end when groups create their final paragraph.

Objective: To summarize the group's thinking on compassion and perseverance through a group writing response activity.

Materials: Pens, markers, large paper clips, chart paper, and reproducible "Comment and Clip It" (page 86)

Directions for facilitated group practice follow.

1. Break into groups of four. Ask each group to select a scribe and speaker. If you are presenting to a large group, groups of eight will work if the members work in pairs when responding to the questions.

2. Place one large paper clip and one copy of "Comment and Clip It" *face down* in the middle of each group of four. Ask them not to turn over the paper until you have given all the directions.

3. Explain that each person's written response will be hidden from others until all four questions have been answered. When an individual has responded to a question, that person folds the paper on the fold line following their question and uses the paper clip to keep it closed.

4. The activity will begin with the person whose birthday (month and day) falls next on the calendar. If there happens to be a tie, the newest member of the staff will begin.

5. After the first person has responded in writing, folded, and clipped their response, they hand the paper to the person on their right. This continues until all four people have completed their responses.

6. The group speaker reads aloud the questions and the responses.

7. The scribe writes the answers to the four questions in a way that creates one paragraph on the chart paper.

8. After all groups have completed writing their paragraph on their chart paper, ask the group speakers to read their paragraphs aloud to the entire group.

9. After all group paragraphs have been read, discuss the common threads that run among the different group responses. The takeaway is realizing some of the most important decisions we make about

students are not about the teaching curriculum. The essence of an educator reveals itself in the responsibility, compassion, and resilience needed for this career.

10. Post these charts in the teachers' lounge. Remind participants of the importance of this topic being a continued conversation.

Directions for independent practice follow.

1. Respond to each question on "Comment and Clip It" one at a time, without looking ahead at the next question.

2. On a separate piece of paper, write your four responses to create a paragraph.

3. Read aloud the paragraph you created and consider the following questions.

   • Do I feel comfortable with my responses?

   • Would I feel comfortable sharing my paragraph with a colleague?

   • How can my responses help me make better decisions in the future?

Try It in the Classroom

The Comment and Clip It activity works best for middle and high school students. Consider using the questions listed here. Follow the facilitated group directions.

• In one sentence, define *compassion* in your own words.

• In one sentence, how does compassion impact others?

• In one sentence, describe what a compassionate classroom looks and feels like to the teacher and to the students.

• In one sentence, explain why intentionally looking for opportunities to demonstrate compassion is important.

This teaching strategy also works to assess the class's comprehension level for any topic.

Next Steps

Slowing down and providing time to reflect demonstrate the value and respect we place on our profession. The authors of the article *Becoming a More Humane Leader* (Hougaard & Carter, 2021) speak to the need to bring one's humanity to leadership: "A good leader values who we are today but also challenges us to stretch ourselves and do better to realize more of our true potential." This rings true for district leaders, campus leaders, department leaders, and classroom leaders. Uninterrupted self-reflection is a rare commodity for educators. Pausing to remember our purpose is invaluable.

Common Questions

Two common questions show up around educator roles: (1) What if I'm not experienced enough to accommodate all my expected roles? and (2) How do I handle feeling burned out from playing so many roles to so many people?

What If I'm Not Experienced Enough to Accommodate All My Expected Roles?

Consider these suggestions if you fear you need more experience.

- **Find a mentor:** Seek out a veteran educator who you know is highly thought of on your campus or department (or even in another building if you work at a small school or are a singleton) and let them know you'd love to learn from them. We sometimes shy away from asking for help because we consider it bothering someone. Most people love to share what they know. Don't be afraid to ask questions and seek their advice. After all:

> When teachers work together, there are more consistencies within schools, with a resultant positive effect on school climate, student engagement, and student learning. Teachers feel confident and are more likely to remain in their chosen profession when they have the support of fellow teachers and work with them closely, collaboratively, and as valued team members. (Vesely, Saklofske, & Leschied, 2013)

- **Ask to be on a committee:** If you are currently not part of a committee and would like to know more about how your campus or department operates, ask if you can sit in on an occasional meeting to listen. You will learn a lot from listening and participating. Being a committee member provides an opportunity to contribute your talent. Every experience we open ourselves to provides an opportunity to learn and grow. Don't sell yourself short—experience comes through doing.

How Do I Handle Feeling Burned Out From Playing So Many Roles to So Many People?

It is not surprising to feel tired or stretched thin at the end of a long day. However, there is a difference between understanding tiredness, stress, or compassion fatigue versus burnout.

> Compassion fatigue is the physical, emotional and psychological impact of supporting others through stressful or traumatic experiences. It is most common in healing and helping professionals like therapists, nurses, doctors, social workers and teachers. If left unaddressed long-term, it could lead to burnout—a long-term onset of hopelessness and feeling like your work has little value or positive impact. (University of Massachusetts Global, n.d.)

Educators hear a lot about self-care, but it is critical to take care of oneself. It might sound simple, and these are habits most people are aware are important, but research proves that it's crucial to prioritize the following actions.

- **Mindfulness** can include meditation, breathwork, or physical fitness—any "activity that helps you to engage in a contemplative thought process and focus on the present moment" (Kolpin, as cited in University of Massachusetts Global, n.d.).

- Get at least seven hours of **sleep** every night.

- **Movement** is beneficial—"decades of research have proven that just 30 minutes of movement a day can have a hugely positive impact on your wellbeing" (Kolpin, as cited in University of Massachusetts Global, n.d.).

- Set and maintain work-life **boundaries**.

- **Ask for help** when you need it, "whether it's from your loved ones, colleagues, a therapist or your supervisor" (Kolpin, as cited in University of Massachusetts Global, n.d.).

Healthy connections with others are critical, since the:

best antidote to burnout . . . is seeking out rich interpersonal interactions and continual personal and professional development. If you band together to offer mutual support, identify problems, and brainstorm and advocate for solutions, you will all increase your sense of control and connection. (Valcour, 2016)

As an administrator, encourage teachers early in their careers to seek out a mentor, or pair them with a more experienced educator. It "makes sense [for newer educators] to take advantage of [more tenured colleagues'] experience and knowledge to help . . . prevent burnout in the earlier stages of their careers" (Bouchrika, 2023).

Also advocate for staff in your building or district in accordance with the research that shows that "higher level of support from school personnel appears to decrease burnout levels" (Park & Shin, 2020, as cited in Bouchrika, 2023). Supporting teachers' decisions, being consistent with decision making (work inequities contribute to burnout; Boushrika, 2023), and monitoring staff for burnout and attending to it when you see it are inexpensive ways to support teachers daily (Education Advanced, 2023). Negative work culture and negative work policies are cited as contributing to burnout (Darbishire, Isaacs, & Miller, 2020). Culture and policies often start with the school's leaders, so make sure to engage teachers in these efforts.

Whether you are a teacher, administrator, counselor, or other educator, develop and maintain strong interpersonal relationships with colleagues. We may spend more time during the work week with our colleagues than we do with our families at home. Keep a sense of humor to keep things in perspective. Laugh with each other. It can be a great stress reliever. Learn from each other. Lean on each other. Most importantly, take care of each other.

Reflection Questions

Consider the following questions, perhaps with a colleague.

- If you've had a mentor in the past, how did the experience help you grow? If you have not had a mentor, who would you seek out to be your mentor and why would you choose that person?

- How would keeping a private journal help you both professionally and personally?

- What recommendations would you give a new teacher just entering the profession?

Mindful and Meaningful Roles

Green: Which role do you play most often? Why?

Blue or purple: When is a time you could have done more for someone, whether a student, family, or friend, by playing a different role? What more could you have done?

Yellow: What role are you best at performing? Why?

Red: What is the hardest decision you have had to make as an educator?

Orange: What role do you find the most difficult? Why?

Brown: What is something you wish a teacher had done for you when you were a student? Have you had the opportunity to do something similar for a student? Explain.

Comment and Clip It

1. In one sentence, define *compassion* in your own words.

Fold Line

2. In one sentence, say how compassion impacts other people.

Fold Line

3. In one sentence, describe what student success looks like.

Fold Line

4. In one sentence, explain why educators don't give up.

Fold Line

CHAPTER 5

Helping High-Mobility Students

When dealing with people, remember you are not dealing
with creatures of logic, but with creatures of emotion.

—DALE CARNEGIE

New students quietly move in and out of schools throughout the year. A ripple occurs. Their empty chair is soon filled by another new student moving into the classroom. If they are lucky, they learn the unspoken class norms and expectations quickly through observation and full immersion.

Throughout the school year, students enroll and withdraw from classrooms, and "these non-promotional school changes are often referred to as student mobility or school mobility" (Rumberger, 2015). There are many reasons students and families may relocate during the school year. Many situations bring with them an already emotionally charged situation. A change in family dynamics, such as divorce or death, a loss of job or promotion, poverty, lack of financial resources to pay upcoming rent, military transfers, purchase of a home, or escaping a dangerous situation are a few examples.

Moving also causes commotion for the receiving teachers and their existing students. Seating arrangements and schedules change, paperwork is added, and groups shift. None of these issues, however, is equivalent to the isolation new students feel as they try to find their place in an established room full of peers who know each other and the teacher: "Students who experienced school changes were more likely to develop antisocial behaviors, less likely to get involved with others, and more likely to avoid classmates" (Han, 2014).

The following vignette is a personal account of how a small gesture, taking only a minute, can make a new student feel seen.

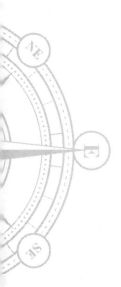

Thank You, Mr. Hutchinson

I changed schools a dozen different times in my life between kindergarten and graduating from high school. I am one of four siblings raised in a military family. With my father serving as an Army soldier, moving is just what we did. My parents made it a point to approach each move as a family adventure to ease the transitions.

When I entered fourth grade, it was the fourth school I attended. Fourth grade was pleasant, as there was no move that year. I was especially happy knowing I would start fifth grade at the same school after the summer break. I had a sense of confidence and comfort knowing I wouldn't be the new kid.

My fifth-grade teacher, Mr. Hutchinson, was tall and skinny and had hair that never stayed in place. I noticed right away that he smiled a lot and laughed easily. I knew this was going to be a great year. I found several of my friends from the previous year. We giggled and waved. September flew by, and I loved being in Mr. Hutchinson's class. He was a kind man who listened and made us work hard but also liked to have fun. October came and went just as fast as September.

Then, it happened. In December, the week before the winter holidays, my parents gathered us around the dining room table to make the big announcement that we were moving back to Texas. I was happy we would be living near my grandparents, but I was sad because I wanted to stay at my current school.

My mom notified the school of when our last day of school would be. On that last day, which came too quickly, I was working on a writing assignment. Mr. Hutchinson walked up, lightly tapped on my desk, lowered his head to look at me, and said, "Gloria, we have really enjoyed having you as a special part of this class. We are going to miss you."

On cue, the students got up from their seats and placed handmade cards on my desk. I remember tears welling up in my eyes.

No teacher, much less a whole class, had ever acknowledged my last day of school before. I changed schools seven more times before graduating from high school, and no other teacher ever again acknowledged my last day. What an act of compassion. Fifty years later, I still smile and get goosebumps remembering that moment. Mr. Hutchinson, wherever you are, thank you!

This chapter talks about some of the issues facing high-mobility students and why we need to be mindful of those issues. The activities help by making participants aware of the many reasons students enter and withdraw from schools and remind us that these multiple moves place stress on the students who deal with them.

Why We Need to Be Mindful of Specific Challenges Related to High Mobility

Repetitive moves affect students in multiple ways, such as creating large academic gaps, social awkwardness, academic insecurity, lack of participation in extracurricular activities, and a higher chance of dropping out of high school. The overall negative impacts of school mobility include social difficulties, classroom disruptions, academic challenges, and impaired school-child relationships (Kokemuller, n.d.).

Research shows that young children, who are still developing at a rapid rate, suffer from disruptions in body and brain development from handling stress over time:

Disruptions in this development can have a snowball effect, which explains how mobility has the potential to harm children . . . . Specifically mobility (particularly repeated mobility) can disrupt children's routines, the consistency of their care and health care, and their relationships, as well as learning routines, relationships with teachers and peers, and the curriculum to which they are exposed. (National Research Council and Institute of Medicine, 2010)

Poorer mental health and poorer academic performance are possible results for those who experience residential mobility, and neither resilience nor family income (which correlates to more resources) mitigate the effects of adolescent residential mobility's poorer academic performance (Li, Li, & Li, 2019). Researchers in Canada find that "mobility in later years [versus] earlier grades also means that dropout can be contemplated as a feasible coping strategy" (Stamp et al., 2022).

Here are some lessons learned.

- **Connect these students with peers:** Researchers suggest that educators "actively help [these students] engage in social activities in school. School administrators may consider establishing a student council to help mobile students learn about the new school and community" (Han, 2014).

- **Help students acknowledge their feelings:** Demonstrate understanding and compassion for what they experience. Make it a priority to approach new students privately and let them know you understand they may be feeling uneasy; tell them how happy you are for them to be a member of the class; and offer to answer any questions or concerns they may have. At the end of their first day, ask how their day was. After the first week, check in to see if they have encountered any issues you can help address. I also suggest calling the students' caregivers at the end of the first week. A brief positive phone call is a perfect way to show you care.

- **Establish traditions, routines, and preparations for when mobile students arrive or depart:** This effort can ease the transition for the student and the campus or class. Creating traditions, such as Mr. Hutchinson did when saying goodbye, becomes the standard way to behave. Once the process is established, it takes very little time to implement and sends an unmistakable sign of caring.

- **Acknowledge mobile students on the day they withdraw:** Showing a withdrawing student that he, she, or they made a difference in your class or school takes little time or money. Even a small recognition— anything with the school logo on it, a handwritten card by the principal or teacher—can create unforgettable moments. Authors Dan and Chip Heath (2017) tell us, "And that's the charge for all of us: to defy the forgettable flatness of everyday work and life by creating a few precious moments" (pp. 265–266).

Tip

The following ideas may help ease student transitions.

- Students entering the school during the school year are provided a scheduled visit with the school counselor during their first week on campus.

- A school administrator can make a follow-up phone call to the parents in the first two to three weeks of entering the new school to inquire how comfortable (or uncomfortable) they feel their child is feeling at the new campus. This action also helps cement a positive school-caregiver relationship (Popp, 2014). (Read more about that in chapter 6, page 105.)

- Assign a buddy for a new student during their first one or two weeks of school. They will have someone to eat lunch with, who will introduce them to their friends, show them the library and the bathrooms, walk with them through crowded halls during passing periods to ensure they get to the correct room, or hang out with them during recess. Almost all teachers—95 percent of them—"say mentors make a difference for students" (De La Rosa, 2022).

- Create routines (such as providing a school tour) when enrolling new students and establish traditions recognizing students who are leaving. These routines and traditions can be campuswide or occur in individual classrooms. Structural routines can help ease the student's transition as well as the staff's efforts in managing the details (Popp, 2014).

- If the school is aware of when a student's last day of school will be, the student receives a check-out interview with the school counselor. Some sample questions follow by grade level.

Elementary school questions follow.

- What is something you will remember about this school that will make you smile?

- What grownups at school could you talk to if you had a problem?

- What would you change about this school to make it better?

Middle school questions follow.

- On a scale of one to ten, with ten being best, how would you rate the friendliest of the students? How would you rate the teachers and principals?

- Did you have specific adults at school you could trust and talk with if you were experiencing problems?

- What would you change about this school to make it better?

High school questions follow.

- On a scale of one to ten, with ten being best, how would you rate the quality of instruction you received at this school?

- Did this school make you feel included? How? If not, how did this school make you feel excluded?

- Were there adults at school you could confide in?

- What is one change you would make to improve this school?

Activities for Understanding the Stressors of High-Mobility Students

The activities in this chapter help to create an understanding of the many reasons students enter and withdraw from schools throughout the school year and remind us that these multiple moves cause additional stress on students. Never underestimate the power schools have on students. Students don't make the decision to relocate. Life situations often dictate hard decisions families must make.

Causes of Student Mobility

Schools experience students enrolling and withdrawing all year. No matter how well planned or how unexpected a move is, each move brings with it a change of teachers, schedules, expectations, transitions, emotions, and friends.

Objective: To identify the difficulties experienced by students when changing schools and share practices that demonstrate compassion and understanding to ease the transition for the student.

Materials: Highlighters, "Thank You, Mr. Hutchinson" vignette (page 88), and reproducible "Causes of Student Mobility" (page 101) (or you can display the questions from step 4 on a large screen for viewing by participants)

Directions for facilitated group practice follow.

1. Read the "Thank You, Mr. Hutchinson" vignette.

2. Break into groups of three or four and provide each group with a copy of the four questions in step 4 to guide their discussions.

3. Pass out copies of "Causes of Student Mobility" and ask participants to read the descriptions. On their own, have participants highlight the bullets they have personally experienced with students on their campus.

4. When participants have finished highlighting, explain that for the next five to seven minutes they will share, in their groups, their personal experiences of receiving new students during the school year. These questions can either be displayed on a large screen or printed on a piece of paper.

   - Were the moves voluntary or involuntary?

   - As the teacher, what difficulties were experienced in transitioning the new student into an already established class?

   - How did the transition affect the class?

   - What accommodations, if any, were made to ease the transition?

5. Engage in whole-group discussion by asking participants what trends they may have noticed.

   - Were some reasons highlighted by everyone in the group?

   - Were there bullets that no one had highlighted?

   - Does this reveal anything about the school community?

6. Establish an intentional system to welcome new students on campus. Ensure that this process is communicated to all personnel. This begins establishing a culture of welcome acceptance for students moving in and out the school's doors.

Directions for independent practice follow.

1. Read "Thank You, Mr. Hutchinson" vignette.

2. In the table of "Causes of Student Mobility," read the differences between voluntary versus involuntary moves.

3. Highlight the bullets on those your students have experienced.

4. Compare the highlighted bullets to those you did not highlight. What does it reveal about your campus?

5. Keep in mind the knowledge of difficulties experienced by new students, the teacher, and the classroom. Set in action specific school or classroom changes to ensure a more compassionate transition.

Being New

Whether arriving at a party or a new job, most people have felt the discomfort of walking into a room full of strangers and everyone watching. Being the center of attention as others size you up is not easy.

Objective: To personally identify the experience of being new at a position and recall what made the participant feel comfortable and welcome, or to identify what could have been done differently to provide a comfortable welcome.

Materials: Chart paper or whiteboard, markers, and the reproducible "Being New" (page 102)

Directions for facilitated group practice follow.

1. Break into groups of three or four and give each participant a copy of "Being New."

2. Explain that even as adults, a move can be scary because we are often afraid of the unknown. Ask participants to close their eyes and think about their first day of teaching or their first day in a new job. Walk them through that day by asking the following questions aloud, slowly.

    • "Were you apprehensive while getting ready in the morning?"

    • "What were you thinking about as you came to work that first day?"

    • "How were you introduced to others?"

- "Did you know the workplace norms and expectations?"

- "Who did you sit with at lunch?"

- "When you left that first day, were you disappointed or pleased? Why?"

3. Read aloud the title of each box on "Being New."

   - First-year teacher

   - First year on grade level or in department

   - First year in a new position

   - Experienced, but new to campus

4. Ask participants to choose the box that applies to a situation they are currently experiencing (or have experienced) and write, in the corresponding box, what made them feel welcome (or what would have made them feel more welcome) during that experience. Give them three minutes to write.

5. When time is called, participants will share their bulleted thoughts with those in their small group.

6. After small groups have finished their conversations, bring their attention to the blank butcher paper on the wall. Ask participants to choose one great idea that came up in their conversation and one person from each group will write the idea on the chart.

7. Read aloud each of the ideas written on the butcher paper. Ask participants to keep the takeaway in mind: acknowledging, even as adults, we feel similar responses to being accepted and welcomed in new situations. Knowing this, it is important to take the initiative to reach out and make others feel welcome and accepted in both personal and professional situations.

Directions for independent practice follow.

1. Have a copy of the reproducible "Being New."

2. Think of an experience you had being new at a job. How did the receiving personnel welcome you (or not welcome you) on the first day?

3. Look at the titles of "Being New."

   - First-year teacher

- First year on grade level or in department

- First year in a new position

- Experienced, but new to campus

4. Choose two boxes that pertain to a situation you have experienced (or are currently experiencing). Bullet your thoughts about what made you feel welcome *or* what could have been done to make you feel more welcome. This should take about three minutes to complete.

5. Compare the differences between the two boxes you chose. Does one stand out as a more positive experience than the other? Why?

6. Choose one great idea from your bullets that you can begin using in your classroom with students or with your grade-level or department team when receiving a new faculty member.

New Kid on the Block

Compassion, no matter how small the action, has a big impact. Moving into a new neighborhood and being greeted by a neighbor who has a smile and a plate of cookies is priceless. Planning inexpensive gestures ahead of time can go a long way in showing compassion, creating connections, and establishing inclusion. What memories can we make for new students entering our schools?

Objective: To create a list of thoughtful ways to welcome students who enter school mid-year.

Materials: Chart paper, markers, and reproducible "New Kid on the Block" (page 103)

Directions for facilitated group practice follow.

1. Break into groups of three or four.

2. Hand out one copy of "New Kid on the Block" to each group and ask someone to read the examples in the Campus and Classroom columns.

3. Explain that this sheet is a template for participants to create their *own* list using the provided chart paper and markers and that they will have fifteen minutes for this task.

4. Have each small group assign a scribe, a materials manager, and two speakers. The duties of the roles are as follows.

- *Scribe* ensures the writing is large and legible.

- *Materials manager* posts the group's chart in the designated area, picks up materials after the activity, and keeps the group on task to ensure they finish in fifteen minutes.

- *Speakers* present the Campus side of the chart and the Classroom side of the chart, one column per speaker.

5. Ask groups to complete their charts.

6. Ask the materials manager to post the chart, then call on each group for its two speakers to present their chart. In a short amount of time, colleagues can generate a full list of ideas that promote acceptance and inclusiveness. It is not difficult or time consuming.

7. Post these charts in the teachers' lounge or another faculty gathering place for the following week to serve as a reminder and motivation.

Directions for independent practice follow.

1. Read "New Kid on the Block."

2. Write at least three more ideas under both columns.

3. Circle one idea on the Campus side you can discuss with your campus administrator within the next two weeks. Circle at least one idea you can commit to incorporating on the Classroom side of the sheet.

4. Be accountable. Many teachers work in teams, departments, or grade levels. These teams usually meet on a regular basis. If your campus is small, you may meet at regular faculty meetings. However your meetings are set up, make sure that the topic of new students is a repeated bullet point on each agenda. Under that subject, list some general questions such as these.

   - Who has received a new student since our last meeting?

   - How do you feel they are adjusting?

   - What extra support does the student or family need?

   - How can someone in this group help ensure this student and family feels included and seen on campus?

5. Knowing this topic will appear regularly on agendas holds everyone accountable and helps ensure that the care and concern of new students remain a priority.

Try It in the Classroom

Students at all grade levels can participate in a teacher-led discussion about student mobility. Invite students to participate in listing ways to welcome new students and ways to say goodbye to students on their last day. In a T-chart, write *Welcome* and *We Will Miss You*. The process of walking students through identifying the need and creating potential actions demonstrates a sense of compassion and requires empathic perspective taking.

Next Steps

Students of high mobility create a subpopulation on the campus that is often overlooked. The emotional stressors carried by students of high mobility may be an invisible fence that is off the radar unless you intentionally look for it. Now that we see it, we can make a difference. We have the potential to impact the culture when our intentions remain student focused.

Common Questions

Three common questions show up around high-mobility students: (1) How do I establish traditions and routines if students often come and go? (2) What if the new student does not engage with other students? and (3) What if we have too many high-mobility students to make this feasible?

How Do I Establish Traditions and Routines If Students Often Show Up and Leave Unexpectedly?

If a student simply leaves without any notice, there will obviously be no chance for an in-person goodbye. However, when an unexpected new student shows up at your door, be ready by doing the following.

- **Prepare informational materials:** Have folders to give them with the class schedule, class rules and expectations, names and contact information for school administration and counselors, a map of the campus, and a campus calendar highlighting annual events and celebrations such as a bookfair, author's visit, school carnival, talent show, field day, and field trips.

- **Drop everything and acknowledge them:** Stop what you are doing; shake the student's hand; welcome him, her, or them; and introduce them to the class. This sounds obvious, but the reason I say this is that as a new student, I was once greeted by a teacher who stopped teaching mid-sentence, pointed to an empty seat in the back of the room, then continued the lesson without missing a beat. It was painfully obvious I was considered an interruption and simply added another body to an already crowded class. More than once as a new student, when being walked to a new classroom by a staff member, I've heard the receiving teacher say, "It's not my turn to get the new kid." Ouch.

What If the New Student Does Not Engage With Other Students?

Peer relationships are important. Social integration is important. Sometimes, students need a little help. Here are some suggestions when helping to integrate new students.

- **Assign a buddy:** Privately ask another student or students to be their lunch buddy, recess buddy, hallway transition buddy, and to go out of their way to include them in group conversations and to introduce them to their group of friends.
- **Initiate a teacher lunch bunch:** Make sure to include the new student in the group. If this is new to you, a lunch bunch is when a teacher has lunch with a group of about three or four randomly selected students. These lunch bunches can be scheduled once a week, once a month, or at specified times throughout the year. Always rotate the students in the group so all students are included.
- **Group carefully:** When assigning the new student to a group project, selectively choose them to be grouped with students who demonstrate kindness and friendliness.
- **Meet with them privately:** After the new student has been in class for a few days, ask if they need anything or how you can make them feel more comfortable.

What If We Have Too Many High-Mobility Students to Make This Feasible?

Your campus may be in a constant state of rotation with students arriving and leaving. By the end of the year, very few students who began the year in your classes might still be in your classroom. This situation may make you feel as if you can't take the time to keep stopping to acknowledge students. However, it provides even more reason to create a campus culture of acknowledging and welcoming highly mobile students. Many students attending campuses such as this often carry additional trauma. Showing a few moments of care and inclusion to these students can go a long way to helping them academically and behaviorally. It is never time wasted.

Reflection Questions

Consider the following questions, perhaps with a colleague.

- Can you think of an instance when a student has withdrawn from your class or school with no acknowledgment? Were you too busy? Did you forget it was their last day? Think about the feelings they may have left with.

- If an involuntary move were to happen in your life and you had no say in the matter, what emotions might you feel?

- The quote from Chip and Dan Heath's (2017) book *The Power of Moments: Why Certain Experiences Have Extraordinary Impact* reads, "What if we didn't just *remember* the defining moments of our lives but *made* them?" serves as a reminder that we have the power to create defining moments for students and their families (italics in original; p. 266). How will you create defining moments for your students and others in your life?

Causes of Student Mobility

Students can move throughout the academic year for many different reasons. Because they are usually minors, the decision to move is normally out of their control.

Read the differences between voluntary and involuntary moves in the table. On your own, highlight the items you have personally experienced. Next, in a small group, share individual experiences with each other focusing on the following bulleted questions.

- Were the students' moves voluntary or involuntary?
- What difficulties were experienced in transitioning the new student into an already established class?
- Was the difficulty in transition just with the new student or did the transition affect the whole class?
- What accommodations, if any, were made to ease the transition?

Voluntary Moves	Involuntary Moves
Usually planned	Usually occurs quickly and without much notice
Preparations take place	Move takes place during time of high emotional stress
Children are made aware of upcoming transition but normally have little to no control over a move	Family may sneak out of current living situation (because they cannot pay rent, for example)
	May leave belongings behind
Sense of control by caregivers	Children may be caught by surprise
	No sense of control by caregivers or children

If you know a student who had to withdraw during the school year for any of the following reasons, highlight those. When completed, share your list with your partners.

Job change
- Promotion
- Caretaker losing job
- Another adult in the home losing income
- Relocating due to military assignment

Change in living arrangements
- Moving in with another family
- Moving to avoid paying rent
- Becoming unhoused
- Finding more affordable housing
- Finding better living accommodations

Change in family structure
- Divorce
- Death

- Foster home placement
- Parent's incarceration
- Parent moves in with new significant other

Escaping a negative social situation
- Gangs and other threats of violence
- Drugs and alcohol in the home or in the community
- Bullying or social exclusion at school
- Immigrants fleeing war or other political unrest
- Unhealthy home situation consisting of physical or emotional abuse

Being New

Choose a box that pertains to a situation you have experienced. Bullet your thoughts about what made you feel welcomed *or* what would have made you feel more welcome.

First-Year Teacher	First Year on Grade Level or in Department
First Year to a New Position	Experienced, but New to Campus

New Kid on the Block

With your team, generate a list of ideas to promote a culture of acceptance and inclusiveness for new students enrolling mid-year.

Campus	Classroom
1. Provide a tour of the campus for caregivers or the student.	1. Assign a new student a daily partner for a week.
2. Provide newly enrolled students a campus gift, such as a magnet with important campus phone numbers, a school pencil, or a welcoming, enthusiastic handwritten letter from another student.	2. Hold a circle meeting where students tell the new student something about themselves.
3. Lunch with, for example, the principal, vice principal, teacher, coach, or school librarian.	3. Lunch with, for example, the principal, vice principal, teacher, coach, or school librarian.
4.	4.
5.	5.
6.	6.

CHAPTER 6

Increasing Caregiver Engagement

Change the way you look at things and the things you look at change.

—WAYNE W. DYER

While preparing a presentation about bridging the gap between home and school with some other educators, we wound up deep in conversation about the barriers to that bridge. A fourth-grade teacher excitedly summed up our conversation by saying, "You know those invisible fences people install in their yards? School barriers are like those invisible fences, only they keep parents from wanting to enter the school." Her perspective continues to provide a vivid mental picture.

The following vignette is an example of stumbling on barriers and creating small changes that lead to big differences.

Paper Bag Lunches

Principal Noris Simmons's school is struggling to engage caregivers. A few weeks into the school year, Principal Simmons receives word that a family specialist will join the faculty. Mrs. Olvera's role is to help increase parent and guardian engagement, provide a variety of classes for them, and connect families with staff at social agencies who can provide an additional system of support.

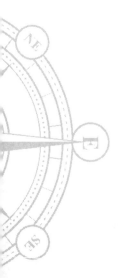

Mrs. Olvera and Principal Simmons quickly begin a meet-and-greet habit of standing on the front steps every morning to get to know the families as they drop off their children. After a few weeks, Principal Simmons asks caregivers about the possibility of them volunteering on campus once a week, explaining that they could change bulletin boards, help younger students in the cafeteria, read to students in various classrooms, deliver items to teachers, or even teach a group of caregivers a new skill. Some respond by saying they can't help because they have younger children.

Principal Simmons asks Mrs. Olvera what she thinks about letting caregivers bring their toddlers with them to her room when they come to volunteer. Parents could rotate watching each other's children on campus while they volunteer during the day.

Without skipping a beat, Mrs. Olvera says, "Let them bring their babies! I've got a corner set up with a rocking chair, and I'll set up a toddler's workstation in another corner. The parents and guardians with little ones would love getting help from the other moms in the room. Let's go for it!"

Initially, three or four parents volunteer every Tuesday.

Principal Simmons notices, however, all but one volunteer leaves just as the cafeteria begins serving the first lunch group. When he asks her where they go, she replies that they go home to eat because a school lunch costs money.

The following week, Principal Simmons, a couple of staff members, and Mrs. Olvera are in her room preparing paper bag lunches as a surprise for the volunteers. Each bag contains a peanut butter and jelly or cheese sandwich, a bag of potato chips, an apple, and a bottle of water. As the volunteers enter the room, they announce, "Please be our guests. This is your room, and this is your private table. Tuesdays lunches are on us. We want to thank you for all you do!"

The volunteers stop in their tracks, look at the sack lunches, look at the staff, and then break out into grins and exclamations of disbelief and thanks.

Three things happened as a result of this gesture: (1) The volunteers started staying through the afternoon, (2) the number of volunteers slowly began to increase, and (3) the lunch bunch bonded and grew into a school family.

It would have been quicker to place a sandwich in a bag and tell parents there are sack lunches available in the parent resource room. It would have been even easier to tell them there was peanut butter in the pantry, jelly in the fridge, and bread on the table if they wanted to fix themselves lunch. But it's all in the details.

> **Tip**
>
> If you try this with your volunteers, you can ask teachers to volunteer their students to decorate the paper bags. Most students enjoy the task. Consider asking students to write notes of appreciation to slip into each bag.

Why We Need to Engage Caregivers

Removing invisible walls and rolling out the welcome mat are steps toward increasing caregiver engagement. If caregivers support a campus, such as by being physically present at school events or volunteering, or if they actively provide academic support and guidance at home, students are the beneficiaries.

For educators to step outside of the schoolyard and venture into the community displays a sense of trust and open arms. When collaboration happens between families and school, student learning and achievement, attitudes toward school, and behavior and social skills improve—and "this holds across families of all economic, ethnic, racial, and educational backgrounds and for students of all ages" (Avnet, Makara, Larwin, & Erickson, 2019). This may not always be an easy task, but if you are lucky enough to visit students in their homes or apartments, you may find you are received like a minor celebrity. Younger siblings who are not yet school age are often intrigued. Stash a few school pencils or stickers in your pocket or bag to give away to these future students. Little things like this make a big difference.

As educators, the messages we send (both verbally and nonverbally) like these, with our actions, can shape the way a district or campus is viewed by its families and the community it serves. Telling and directing families may be interpreted as a hierarchy of social power or can alienate. As an alternative, "rather than decide for, [instead] inform, and teach families . . . consult and partner with them" (Radd, Gooden, Generett, & Theoharis, 2022). Sharon Radd and colleagues (2022), in their research, go on to say, "Like all good leaders, school leaders in an equity-focused partnership must be empathetic and compassionate in their view of, and interactions with families, and 'conflict competent.'" When both the caregivers and educators share knowledge in making decisions in the best interest of the student, everyone wins—the school, the caregivers, and most importantly, the student.

We cannot do the important job of school leadership to its fullest without the support of student caregivers and communities. Removing barriers for the parents and community of our schools is equivalent to rolling out the welcome mat in our home. A study from the *International Journal of Evaluation and Research in Education* (Avnet et al., 2019) reveals that "Parental involvement can make an impact on the community through parental networking and can improve the interactions between the school and family." It also impacts students: "Students' attitudes and behaviors improve, students' competence, grades, test scores, and attendance increase, and they develop better social skills and self-confidence" (Loeza, 2021, p. 3). The message is clear: *Please, join us.*

Here are some lessons learned.

- **Be open about who and what school engagement looks like:** Many elements affect how and when caregivers engage with their charge's school. In addition to asking caregivers to provide help, consider other avenues of engagement, such as the following.

    - Pair high school students with elementary school students to act as reading buddies.

    - Bring experiences onto the campus, such as visits from authors, artists, musicians, dancers, and poets.

    - Enlist local leaders to participate in on-campus career fairs as early as elementary school (including local tradespeople and professionals) to speak with students about career possibilities.

    - At the secondary level, ask local businesses to consider establishing a partnership of extended school learning through real-life learning opportunities, including inviting classes to visit their establishment to learn about their business or offering internships or part-time jobs to students.

- **Take care of volunteers:** The school benefits, students benefit, and families benefit when caregivers volunteer. Volunteers share the experience of working with others for a common goal and have their voices heard. A study points out that caregiver volunteers recognize:

the importance of building a community where parents and teachers feel honored, appreciated, and respected; of parents feeling empowered to actively participate in school decision-making; and working as a team to support children's learning all point to a model in which parents are part of a school community that supports all of its members. (Gross et al., 2020)

- **Listen to parents:** Let them know their voice counts. They are an important part of the three-legged stool needed to create a successful school environment for students that includes (1) the caregivers, (2) the school, and (3) the students themselves. Consider the following, for example:

  > Rather than interpreting parental absences as a lack of commitment to their children's education, ask families what you can do to support an ongoing partnership. Phone conferences might be a good alternative. Initiating an interactive journal with the parent about what's happening at school and at home could help with teacher–parent dialogue. (Moore, 2013, p. 10)

Activities for Engaging Caregivers

The following activities highlight the importance of being intentional. None of us are immune to being left out or not knowing how to connect. Participants will share their personal experiences and brainstorm ideas to prevent causing unintentional exclusion.

Taking Down the Invisible Fence

It is easy to go about our daily routine just accepting the way things have always been. It takes intentionality to discover invisible fences or barriers we have never noticed. The first step is becoming aware of our barriers. The second step is making a positive effort to eliminate these barriers.

Objective: To define what an invisible fence is, recognize invisible fences on campus, and create a more inclusive environment for families.

Materials: Highlighters, "Paper Bag Lunches" vignette (page 105), and reproducible "Taking Down the Invisible Fence" (page 120)

Directions for facilitated group practice follow.

1. Read aloud the "Paper Bag Lunches" vignette.

2.   Give each participant a highlighter and a copy of "Taking Down the Invisible Fence."

3.   Ask participants to read each statement silently and highlight the statements they have personally experienced or witnessed.

4.   When participants are finished highlighting, ask them to turn to a partner (in groups of two or three) and discuss what they have highlighted.

5.   Ask for volunteers to share a few of their experiences.

6.   Engage participants in reflection not by asking them to verbally respond but to ask themselves if there are highlighted statements on the paper occurring on their campus. If so, how can they be a positive change agent?

Moving forward, be a change agent. Here is a step-by-step example of how to move forward.

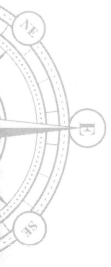

1.   Choose one highlighted item that you have experienced as a barrier on your campus or department.

2.   Find one or two like-minded colleagues with whom you can form a team.

3.   Together, brainstorm suggestions for modifications or alternatives to the current barrier.

4.   Determine which school leader can address the possibility of implementing this change and arrange a date to meet with them.

5.   Share the importance of removing barriers and present your ideas for creating this positive change.

Directions for independent practice follow.

1.   Read the "Paper Bag Lunches" vignette.

2.   Read each statement on the reproducible "Taking Down the Invisible Fence" and highlight those you have personally experienced or witnessed.

3.   Are any of the highlighted statements on your paper occurring where you work? If so, how can you be a positive change agent?

4.   Moving forward, be a change agent with the steps provided for group work.

> ### Tip
>
> Find a buddy or two who will work with you to take action. Gallup CEO Jon Clifton (2022) describes the collaboration of work friends: "When people share a common goal and achieve great things together, they form a connection. The joy is in working together to produce magic." Accomplishing a task as a team has several benefits: "When working together on a common goal or deliverable as an integrated whole, individual members consistently encourage and support each another. Indeed, one of the most prized benefits of good teamwork is a reduction in perceived work stress" (It's Your Yale, n.d.).

Making Magic

We have all heard the saying, *If we always do what we've always done, we will always get what we've always got.* If things are not working, quit doing them the same way or quit doing them altogether. Begin creating change where you see it is needed.

Objective: To work collaboratively and "make magic" by identifying improvements for stale or outdated practices and then, as a team, take action steps for accountability of creating positive change.

Materials: Pens, markers, tape or other means of securing posters to walls, chart paper, and reproducible "Making Magic" (page 121)

Directions for facilitated group practice follow.

1. Break into groups of four and ask each to assign a scribe, artist, timekeeper, and presenter.

2. Provide each *participant* with a pen and a copy of "Making Magic." Provide each *group* with one piece of chart paper and several markers.

3. As a whole group, discuss the example provided on "Making Magic." Ask the following questions.

   - "How can we take any ordinary, sometimes overlooked event or occasion and make it extra special?"

   - "What small tweaks can be made to make it inviting and memorable?"

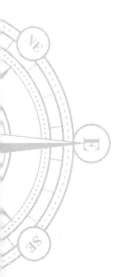

Share examples, which include personalized invitations, colorful balloons, nametags, room decor, student roles as parent guides, refreshments, and personalized follow-up thank-you notes.

4. Tell participants they are to agree on one invisible fence or stale practice. They will collaboratively use their magic to create a fresh, positive spin on their chosen invisible fence or stale practice, jotting ideas on their own copies of "Making Magic" as they brainstorm.

5. The group will then work together for thirty minutes to transfer their ideas, notes, and drawings to their posters. Encourage groups to be as creative as possible.

6. When posters are finished, have the group tape and display them on a wall.

7. After time is called, call upon each group's presenter to share their idea with the whole group.

8. Challenge participants not to let their ideas drop here. Ask them to continue the work by creating a detailed plan that includes the rationale behind the proposed changes, as well as a list of the suggested changes or additions to the status quo. Once they create a plan, make an appointment to present it to the leaders in charge of this area of decision making. I have found it is best to have an answer or solution in hand when presenting a problem or suggesting changes to a current practice. Be able to explain how the change can make a positive impact.

9. Following this, ask for your small group to be placed on the agenda for the next meeting of the event you are improving; once you present, volunteer you and your team to be involved in the planning, preparation, and implementation of the improvements for the identified event.

Directions for independent practice follow.

1. Look at the reproducible "Making Magic."

2. Think of one invisible fence or stale practice at your workplace.

3. Use the given space on "Making Magic" to jot down your ideas and notes.

4. Create your poster with your ideas, notes, and drawings to make a positive change.

5. Share with a colleague, work friend, or boss when possible.

6. Create a written plan to implement your ideas, including a description of the benefits and the potential positive outcomes. Present this plan to whatever body has decision-making power.

From the Outside In

In the words of actor Amy Poehler (2011), "Find a group of people who challenge and inspire you, spend a lot of time with them, and it will change your life." I would also add that it can change the lives of others. When we feel challenged and inspired, we bring that energy into our work and into the classrooms. We spread our enthusiasm and influence the future with how we model acceptance and inclusion of all who walk through our doors.

Objective: To remind participants that, even as adults, the feeling of exclusion can linger and to imprint the need for educator awareness of creating schools and classrooms which are spaces of inclusion and acceptance. This activity works best with groups of no fewer than six people, so requires quite a few participants.

Materials: Whistle or another noisemaker, timer, sticky notes, a large sheet of butcher paper, pens, a room large enough for small groups to face each other, "Paper Bag Lunches" vignette, the reproducibles "Knee to Knee" (page 122) and "Facilitator Directions for From the Outside In Activity" at **go.SolutionTree.com/ teacherefficacy**

Directions for facilitated group practice follow.

1. Read the "Paper Bag Lunches" vignette.

2. Give each participant a sticky note and a copy of "Knee to Knee."

3. Provide between three and five minutes for participants to think about the questions on "Knee to Knee" and write notes on their paper. Remind participants of how the volunteers in the "Paper Bag Lunches" vignette may have felt when they left campus for lunch. Participants will take "Knee to Knee" with them when they break into groups.

4. Break into groups of eight, ten, or twelve, since only even numbers will work for this activity.

5. For each group, line up chairs across from each other. For example, if there are ten people in each small group, each group will have two rows of five chairs facing each other. You can arrange chairs

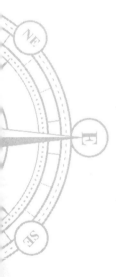

in advance or ask groups to move their chairs with them to a specific area.

6. Once the participants are in their groups, ask them to number off one and two. The row of ones faces the row of twos.

7. Let participants know that the person they're facing is their partner and that each facing partner has one minute to share their thoughts and responses from their completed "Knee to Knee." The ones participants talk first.

8. Sound a signal for the ones to begin sharing. After one minute, the presenter signals for the twos to begin sharing. After a minute, sound the signal to stop the sharing.

9. After each round of sharing, ask the ones to remain seated throughout the activity. Ask the twos to move to the right one seat in their row. Now everyone has a new partner. Rounds continue until all ones and twos have shared with each other.

10. Ask participants to write a word, phrase, or sentence on their sticky notes about how this activity left them feeling.

11. Ask participants to place their sticky notes on the butcher paper and display it for the remainder of the meeting. Now, participants have a better understanding that memories of feeling left out are not easily forgotten. They linger with us.

Directions for independent practice follow.

1. Write your responses to the questions on "Knee to Knee."

2. Write a word, phrase, or sentence on the sticky note about how being *included* in an event, group, organization, or activity made you feel.

3. Keep this note in a place you view often to remind yourself to intentionally create places of inclusion and compassion.

Examples of action steps follow.

- Establish a Buddy Bench outside the classroom. This designated place is where students choose to sit if they are wanting someone to play with or talk with. It is important to note that this entails conversations with the class to ensure all students understand this is to be seen as a chance to demonstrate friendship and compassion with classmates.

- Establish a corner of the classroom (or make it a separate section of your classroom library) to house grade-level books on kindness, inclusion, and acceptance. Refer to the lessons these books contain.

- Lead your students in creating a class motto about acceptance. Together, list examples of how students can demonstrate acceptance and inclusion at school. Post both the motto and the list of examples on the classroom wall. Regularly refer to them so they become part of the classroom culture.

- Partner with students who have special needs so students jointly work together on projects three or four times a year.

- Recognize students who demonstrate acts of acceptance and inclusion.

The Family Room

The thought and detail put into the creation of a family room speaks volumes about the school's attitude toward its families. This family room should serve several functions: this is where classes will be held for parents, where confidential conferences will take place, and where parents will create friendships with other parents. It is important for this room to serve as a safe space where parents want to come. This is where the invisible fence between home and school disappears. This is an opportunity to send a clear message to your community, *We believe in you and your family. This is* your *school. We welcome you.*

The creation of a campus family room may entail the joint effort of an entire campus or the creation of a specific committee assigned to the task. As with students, create an environment for families that is welcoming and pleasant to inspire and motivate. Studies indicate high-quality classroom environments "help children feel safe, secure, and valued. As a result, self-esteem increases, and students are motivated to engage in the learning process" (Reinisch, as cited in SHARE Team, 2012). Tiny differences can make a big impact in the classroom.

The goal of putting extra effort into creating a warm and inviting family room is for families to feel they have a comfortable, safe place where they are valued. They are encouraged to feel ownership and belonging.

Objective: To create a space of warmth and acceptance that welcomes all school families while being intentionally aware of the needs, cultures, and customs of the community to erase invisible barriers.

Materials: Usable items in good shape from home, tag sales, and donations and the reproducible "Creating a Family Room: Checklist" (page 123)

Directions for practice follow. There are no separate directions for group and independent practice.

1. Break participants into committees that are responsible for certain aspects of the room. Responsibilities and roles may include hanging curtains, organizing bins, creating a coffee area, finding the furniture, painting the room, arrangement of spaces—such as instructional area, craft area, area for storage of clothing collection, space for food closet, and sitting area (with couch) or reception area. The spaces will be determined by the amount of room available.

2. Visit the available spaces, including empty classrooms, outbuildings, and portable buildings, to choose the family room location.

3. Seek item donations from faculty, school families, businesses, and charities.

4. When the room is complete, hold a soft open house for the faculty and staff so they get a preview of the finished room before the official opening.

5. Hold a public open house. Make it special by inviting all caregivers and staff. Consider having a ribbon cutting, refreshments, and a short dedication speech. Celebrate!

Next Steps

Compassion sometimes means opening our eyes and noticing what others walk past. Think of the messages people get when litter is not picked up, a marquis has missing letters, groups (either students or adults) are exclusionary, or students and caregivers aren't received with a smile, welcome gesture, or an interpreter when necessary.

Four paradigm shifts can create more inclusivity for caregivers and families (Radd et al., 2022).

1. **Change how you engage with families:** For example, employ translators whenever possible, provide multilingual newsletters, conduct home visits, and offer virtual conferences if that fits the family's needs.

2. **Instead of focusing on what isn't happening, focus on what caregivers have to offer or can do:** This includes treating caregivers as partners and keeping the fact that we have much to learn from families front of mind (Radd et al., 2022).

3. **Use your power for good:** Amplify families' voices whenever you can. Include families' needs, opinions, and perspectives so their influence is considered during decision making.

4. **Remember that socioeconomic need doesn't mean a family isn't competent in all ways:** They need certain materials and items, but that is not equivalent to lacking warmth, intelligence, rich experiences, and a bevy of interpersonal skills (Radd et al., 2022).

Compassion is at the heart of each one of these shifts.

Common Questions

Common questions show up around caregiver engagement: (1) How do we make change when we lack the budget? (2) How do we handle naysayers? and (3) Who should we include on the team when creating the campus family room?

How Do We Make Change When We Lack the Budget ?

Make connections with the managers of local businesses. Let them know how you are trying to improve the school and community. Don't be afraid to ask for donations. Local hardware stores, grocery stores, restaurants, and big-box stores often want to partner with a campus. Often items will be given to schools at big discounts or for free.

For example, I once ran a summer program and had no money budgeted to provide students with something to eat in the mornings. I stopped by a local donut shop (that I often stopped at for myself on the way to work) and explained the situation to the manager. He said that every morning we could have all the donuts that were left from the previous day—for free! Every morning on my way to work, I received about six dozen delicious donuts for the students.

We asked the students to write thank-you notes, and I hand delivered them to the bakery. The next morning, I saw the notes posted all over the bakery walls. It was a win-win situation, and all it took was asking.

How Do We Handle Naysayers?

Naysayers typically believe that if the school focuses solely on academics, then everything else will fall into place. Not everyone agrees that time should be spent on what naysayers call *fluff*, such as building connections, strengthening relationships, and tearing down invisible walls.

This may sound harsh but ignore the naysayers. Focus on the energy coming from faculty and staff who believe students and families thrive (both academically and emotionally) from caring, compassionate, and inclusive connections. Look for those who are willing to put in the work to create positive change. Provide opportunities for this group to work together and let their attitude and effort be the impetus for change. Recognize them, listen to their ideas, and applaud their efforts.

Naysayers will be overshadowed by the energy, commitment, and enthusiasm of these teacher leaders. After standing on the sidelines watching incremental successes, they may start believing. You may even win over a few. Welcome them with open arms.

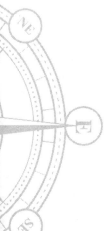

Who Should We Include on the Team When Creating a Campus Family Room?

Since creating a family room is normally considered a campus initiative, this working group should consist of a variety of members representing different departments. This allows for diverse perspectives and ideas. Consider inviting people from the following groups to participate in one way or another.

- **Administrators:** This is usually the principal or assistant principal. They have power over the budget and final call on items that may need approval.

- **Counselors:** Many school counselors have background knowledge in creating calm, trusting environments.

- **Family specialists or social workers:** Different districts use these terms interchangeably. These people are familiar with family and community needs, the available services in the area, and activities or classes that may take place in this designed space.

- **Teachers:** Include teachers from various grade levels or departments. If they have been on campus for a few years, these teachers may have taught a string of siblings and possibly even the parents of siblings.

These relationships bring a wealth of knowledge about the history of the needs of families in the community. New teachers, on the other hand, contribute their unbiased views, along with the views of a younger generation.

- **Caregivers:** Always include caregivers on the development team. They are the voice of your community. Caregivers include parents, but the term *caregiver* also includes others who may be involved in raising a child—grandparents, stepparents, foster parents, or aunts and uncles. Often, a local community contact provides after-school care in their home for many of the families in the area. They may be someone to consider asking to share their expertise with the team.

- **Local business owners:** These people often have many connections in the area. They may offer to provide donations or know people who would be willing to contribute to your cause. A thriving school makes for a thriving community. Thriving communities attract more business. It creates a win-win situation.

Reflection Questions

Consider the following questions, perhaps with a colleague.

- Have you ever been considered a naysayer when a change was implemented? What kept you from wanting change or believing it could be done?

- What roadblock to change is the hardest to overcome?

- Have you ever thought, "We do it this way because we've always done it this way"? If so, what is the rationale for doing something a new way? If not, how do you feel when you hear that from a colleague?

Taking Down the Invisible Fence

Read each statement. Highlight the invisible fences you have experienced or witnessed.

- Signs written in negative language

- Students' parents being perceived by educators as subordinates rather than partners

- Interpreters not being available for meetings with families who speak a language other than English

- Written communication sent to families only in English (if the campus serves a population that speaks other languages)

- Caregivers not being allowed to check out books from the campus library

- Caregiver classes being scheduled at times best suited for the school's convenience, not for the caregivers' convenience

- A lack of effort in establishing relationships with families because of the mistaken belief that parents and guardians don't care

- Educators using educational acronyms and esoteric language when speaking with caregivers

- Lack of effort to learn the stories of the families served

- A low-income campus asking students to donate food for a food drive

Making Magic

Campus Practice	Describe Invisible Fences	Making Magic— Vision Board
Example: Parent attendance at the monthly principal chats is very low. • Monthly notices are sent through an online newsletter. • These monthly events are scheduled for 10:00 a.m. • RSVPs are required.	Example: Invisible fences • Notices are sent only online, and some families may not have access to technology. • The time of day for the chats may not be best for parents. • Some families may hesitate to RSVP if their schedule fluctuates because that makes it hard to commit.	Example: Magic • Have a canopy or table set up in front of the school as parents arrive with their children in the morning. • Decorate with balloons and a sign that reads, *Come join me for a donut after the bell rings!* Serve donuts, coffee, and juice. • Have a sign-in sheet so caregivers may receive a thank-you postcard after attending that requests their attendance at the next monthly principal chat.

Knee to Knee

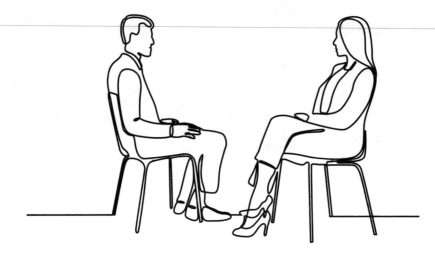

Think of a time, personally or professionally, when you felt excluded (such as not being invited to a special event or group happy hour, not being asked to be a member of a committee, being unaware of an inside joke, not being asked to eat lunch with others, or realizing that others stopped talking when you entered a room).

What did you see or hear (or *not* see or hear) that made you feel excluded?

What would have made you feel more included?

Creating a Family Room: Checklist

Location

Think about the following criteria when choosing a location.

- [ ] Easily accessible (as close to the front of campus as possible)
- [ ] Set up more as a cozy home instead of a schoolroom or office
- [ ] Away from louder areas, such as the cafeteria or band hall
- [ ] Access to a sink and a bathroom (away from student bathrooms)
- [ ] Has a closet for storage
- [ ] Large enough to arrange tables to teach parent classes

This space might work:

Suggested Items for Set-Up

- Refrigerator
- Coffee maker
- Microwave
- Full-length mirror (to enhance students' positive self-images)
- Washer and dryer
- Round tables (to encourage more intimate communication)
- Seating with a couch and small table
- Seasonal tablecloths (inexpensive plastic works)

- Curtains on windows
- Meaningful pictures, inspirational signs, or quotes
- Clear plastic labeled storage bins for the items listed in the Organization section.
- Small children's table and chairs in a corner for parents who bring young children to meetings
  - Coloring books and crayons
  - Books
  - Toys

Organization

Organization is important. When the room is clean and organized, it reflects that someone cares about it. Buy or seek donations for materials that will keep the following items in their proper places and easy to locate.

- Clothing
- Shoes
- School supplies
- Backpacks
- Toys and books
- Craft supplies
- Food and beverages

- Plates, cups, silverware, and napkins
- Paperwork
- Parent resource materials
- Hygiene items (in small baggies)
- Seasonal decorations

Conclusion

*Growing children with an inner compass that
guides their steps toward kindness and compassion
and generosity of spirit is far, far and away superior
to training children to operate on automatic pilot.*

—L. R. KNOST

Being accountable for students does not mean seeing them as a score on an achievement test. Being accountable for students means caring enough to see them as the unique individuals they are. Understanding that a nonjudgmental environment of empathy and compassion can enhance a student's ability to be successful provides a path for us to follow.

Looking through the eyes of intentional awareness, opportunities for compassion appear everywhere. How often do we *intend* to do the little things for people in our lives that may make a big difference but forget or get too busy? We were not intentional about making the person a priority. We've all said, "I intended to do that but . . . ." Acts of compassion can be taught and are skills that can be improved with practice. My dad repeated this maxim many times: "The road to hell is paved with good intentions." In other words, intending to do something is not good enough. We must *act* on our good intentions.

Educators hold significant power in creating lasting impressions on the lives of students. They give students a compass to guide their actions and thoughts toward compassion. Inspiring them to understand the value of empathy and compassion involves engaging both their hearts and their minds. Students hear what we say but remember what we do and how we make them feel. When students feel seen, accepted, included, and validated they are positioned to reach their highest potential.

This book is a call to action. Use this book as an entry point to reach and teach all students through empathy, inclusion, and compassion. Let us shine a light on their internal compass and guide them toward a path of developing compassion for others.

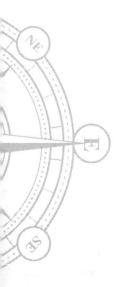

REFERENCES AND RESOURCES

AAA Native Arts. (2022). *Walk a mile in his moccasins.* Accessed at www.aaanativearts .com/walk-mile-in-his-moccasins on April 7, 2023.

Abramson, A. (2021). *Cultivating empathy: Psychologists' research offers insight into why it's so important to practice the "right" kind of empathy, and how to grow these skills.* Accessed at www.apa.org/monitor/2021/11/feature-cultivating-empathy on May 12, 2023.

Alisic, E., Bus, M., Dulack, W., Pennings, L., & Splinter, J. (2012). Teachers' experiences supporting children after traumatic exposure. *Journal of Traumatic Stress, 25*(1), 98–101.

Avnet, M., Makara, D., Larwin, K. H., & Erickson, M. (2019). The impact of parental involvement and education on academic achievement in elementary school. *International Journal of Evaluation and Research in Education (IJERE), 8*(3), 476–483.

Bouchrika, I. (2023). *Teacher burnout statistics: Challenges in K–12 and higher education.* Accessed at https://research.com/education/teacher-burnout-challenges-in-k-12-and -higher-education on May 16, 2023.

Brower, T. (2021). *Empathy is the most important leadership skill according to research.* Accessed at www.forbes.com/sites/tracybrower/2021/09/19/empathy-is-the-most -important-leadership-skill-according-to-research/?sh=5dd2123f3dc5 on April 7, 2023.

Burnett, D. (2018). *Happy brain: Where happiness comes from, and why.* New York: W.W. Norton & Company.

Cacciatore, G. (2021). Teacher-student relationships matter. *Usable Knowledge.* Accessed at www.gse.harvard.edu/news/uk/21/03/teacher-student-relationships-matter on June 14, 2023.

Casas, J. (2017). *Culturize: Every student. Every day. Whatever it takes*. San Diego, CA: Dave Burgess Consulting.

Cherry, K. (2023). What is empathy? *Verywell Mind*. Accessed at www.verywellmind .com/what-is-empathy-2795562 on June 10, 2023.

Clifton, J. (2022). The power of work friends. *Harvard Business Review*. Accessed at https://hbr.org/2022/10/the-power-of-work-friends on May 16, 2023.

Cuadrado, I., Ordóñez-Carrasco, J. L., López-Rodríguez, L., Vázquez, A., & Brambilla, M. (2021). Tolerance towards difference: Adaptation and psychometric properties of the Spanish version of a new measure of tolerance and sex-moderated relations with prejudice. *International Journal of Intercultural Relations*. Accessed at www.sciencedirect.com/science/article/pii /S014717672100119X on May 16, 2023.

Darbishire, P., Isaacs, A. N., & Miller, M. L. (2020). Faculty burnout in pharmacy education. *American Journal of Pharmaceutical Education, 84*(7). https://doi .org/10.5688/ajpe7925

De La Rosa, S. (2022). 95% of teachers say mentors make a difference for students. *K–12 Dive*. Accessed at www.k12dive.com/news/95-of-teachers-say-mentors -make-a-difference-for-students/617250 on May 15, 2023.

DeSteno, D. (2018). *How to cultivate gratitude, compassion, and pride on your team*. Accessed at www.hbr.org/2018/02/how-to-cultivate-gratitude-compassion-and -pride-on-your-team on April 7, 2023.

Dr. Seuss. (1971). *The Lorax*. New York: Random House.

Dubin, A. (2022). Signs that you might be trauma-dumping instead of just venting, according to psychologists. *Insider*. Accessed at www.insider.com/guides/health /mental-health/trauma-dumping May 14, 2023.

Eanes, R. (2021, December 27). Your words affect your child's brain [Blog post]. *Generation Mindful*. Accessed at https://genmindful.com/blogs/mindful -moments/your-words-affect-your-child-s-brain on April 7, 2023.

Education Advanced. (2023, December 23). *10 ways a principal can support teachers* [Blog post]. Accessed at https://educationadvanced.com/resources/blog/10-ways -a-principal-can-support-teachers on July 17, 2023.

Fiarman, S. E. (2016). Unconscious bias: When good intentions aren't enough. *Educational Leadership, 74*(3), 10–15.

Fleming, N. (2020). *6 exercises to get to know your students better—and increase their engagement*. Accessed at www.edutopia.org/article/6-exercises-get-know-your- students-better-and-increase-their-engagement on August 2, 2023.

Flook, L. (2019). *Four ways schools can support the whole child*. Accessed at https:// greatergood.berkeley.edu/article/item/four_ways_schools_can_support_the _whole_child on July 15, 2023.

Ge, Y., Li, W., Chen, F., Kayani, S., & Qin, G. (2021). The theories of the development of students: A factor to shape teacher empathy from the perspective of motivation. *Frontiers in Psychology, 12.*

Gino, F., & Coffman, K. (2021). Unconscious bias training that works. *Harvard Business Review.* Accessed at https://hbr.org/2021/09/unconscious-bias-training -that-works on May 15, 2023.

Goodall, J., & Montgomery, C. (2014). Parental involvement to parental engagement: A continuum. *Educational Review, 66*(4), 399–410. Accessed at http://dx.doi.org /10.1080/00131911.2013.781576 on April 7, 2023.

Greater Good in Education. (n.d.). *2 x 10: Getting to know a student.* Accessed at https://ggie.berkeley.edu/practice/2-x-10-getting-to-know-your-students on May 15, 2023.

Greater Good Magazine. (n.d.). *What is compassion?* Accessed at https://greatergood. berkeley.edu/topic/compassion/definition#:~:text=Compassion%20is%20not%20 the%20same,include%20the%20desire%20to%20help on May 15, 2023.

Gross, D., Bettencourt, A. F., Taylor, K., Francis, L., Bower, K., & Singleton, D. L. (2020). What is parent engagement in early learning? Depends on who you ask. *Journal of Child and Family Studies, 29,* 747–760.

Han, S. (2014). School mobility and students' academic and behavioral outcomes. *International Journal of Education Policy and Leadership, 9*(6). doi: https://doi .org/10.22230/ijepl.2014v9n6a573.

Harvard Health. (2020). *Understanding the stress response: Chronic activation of this survival mechanism impairs health.* Accessed at www.health.harvard.edu/staying -healthy/understanding-the-stress-response on April 18, 2023.

Harvard Kennedy School. (n.d.). *Using small groups to engage students and deepen learning in new HKS classrooms.* Accessed at www.hks.harvard.edu/sites/default /files/Academic%20Dean's%20Office/Guide%20to%20Small-Group%20 Learning.pdf on July 16, 2023.

Harvard School of Public Health. (n.d.). *Understanding unconscious bias.* Accessed at www.hsph.harvard.edu/wp-content/uploads/sites/2597/2022/06/Types-of-Bias -Ways-to-Manage-Bias_HANDOUT-1.pdf on July 16, 2023.

Hasell, J., Roser, M., Ortiz-Ospina, E., & Arriagada, P. (2022). Poverty. *Our World in Data.* Accessed at https://ourworldindata.org/poverty on May 15, 2023.

Heath, C., & Heath, D. (2017). *The power of moments: Why certain experiences have extraordinary impact.* New York: Simon and Schuster.

Hillis, S., Mercy, J., Amobi, A., & Kress, H. (2016). Global prevalence of past-year violence against children: A systematic review and minimum estimates. *Pediatrics, 137*(3), 1–13.

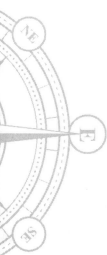

Hougaard, R. (2020). *Four reasons why compassion is better for humanity than empathy.* Accessed at www.forbes.com/sites/rasmushougaard/2020/07/08/four-reasons-why-compassion-is-better-for-humanity-than-empathy/?sh=3e81fa2dd6f9 on April 7, 2023.

Hougaard, R., & Carter, J. (2021). *Becoming a more humane leader.* Accessed at https://hbr.org/2021/11/becoming-a-more-humane-leader on April 7, 2023.

Huddy, S. (2015). Vulnerability in the classroom: Instructor's ability to build trust impacts the student's learning experience, *International Journal of Education Research, 10*(2), 96–103.

It's Your Yale. (n.d.). *We know teamwork is important, but how important?* Accessed at https://your.yale.edu/we-know-teamwork-important-how-important on June 23, 2023.

Kahlenberg, R. D., & Potter, H. (2014). *Why teacher voice matters.* Accessed at www.aft.org/ae/winter2014-2015/kahlenberg_potter_sb on July 16, 2023.

Keys, D. (1982). *Earth at Omega: Passage to planetization.* Boston: The Branden Press.

K.N.C. (2019). How to increase empathy and unite society. *The Economist.* Accessed at www.economist.com/open-future/2019/06/07/how-to-increase-empathy-and-unite-society on June 10, 2023.

Kokemuller, N. (n.d.). *The negative impact of children changing schools.* Accessed at https://education.seattlepi.com/negative-impact-children-changing-schools-2011.html on June 15, 2023.

Kurland, B. (2019, September 18). Beyond empathy: The power of compassion [Blog post]. *Psychology Today.* Accessed at www.psychologytoday.com/us/blog/the-well-being-toolkit/201909/beyond-empathy-the-power-compassion on November 28, 2022.

Lan, Y. (2022). The role of teachers' grit and motivation in self-directed professional development. *Frontiers in Psychology.* Accessed at www.frontiersin.org/articles/10.3389/fpsyg.2022.922693/full on July 17, 2023.

Lathrap, M. T. (1895). *Rare gems from the literary works of Mary T. Lathrap: Born April 25, 1838, died January 3, 1895.* Cleveland, OH: Woman's Christian Temperance Union.

Leonard, J. (2020). *What is trauma? What to know.* Accessed at www.medicalnewstoday.com/articles/trauma on July 15, 2023.

Lesser, M. (2019). *Seven practices of a mindful leader: Lessons from Google and a Zen monastery kitchen.* Novato, CA: New World Library.

Li, M., Li, W., & Li, L. M. W. (2019). Sensitive periods of moving on mental health and academic performance among university students. *Frontiers in Psychology 10.* Accessed at www.ncbi.nlm.nih.gov/pmc/articles/PMC6585164 on May 14, 2023.

Loeza, S. (2021). *Increasing parent involvement for low-income, multilingual parents.* Accessed at https://scholarworks.calstate.edu/downloads/3n204433p on May 15, 2023.

Lonczak, H. S. (2019). 20 reasons why compassion is so important in psychology. *Positive Psychology.* Accessed at https://positivepsychology.com/why-is-compassion-important on July 16, 2023.

Longobardi, C., Prino, L. E., Marengo, D., & Settanni, M. (2016). Student-teacher relationships as a protective factor for school adjustment during the transition from middle to high school. *Frontiers in Psychology.* Accessed at www.ncbi.nlm.nih.gov/pmc/articles/PMC5179523 on May 15, 2023.

Lowrie, L. (2019). Vulnerability in the classroom. *Faculty Focus.* Accessed at www.facultyfocus.com/articles/teaching-and-learning/vulnerability-in-the-classroom on May 14, 2023.

Lynch, M. (2016). *The power of parents: A primer on parental involvement.* Accessed at www.theedadvocate.org/power-parents-primer-parental-involvement on April 7, 2023.

Malone, C., & Fiske, S. T. (2013). *The human brand: How we relate to people, products, and companies.* San Francisco: Jossey-Bass.

McIntosh, P. (1989). White privilege: Unpacking the invisible knapsack. In S. Plous (Ed.), *Understanding prejudice and discrimination* (pp. 191–196). New York: McGraw-Hill.

McNinch, J. (2022). *Parent teacher home visits initiative final report.* Accessed at https://saskschoolboards.ca/wp-content/uploads/SSBA-PTHV-Initiative-Final-Report.pdf on July 16, 2023.

Miller, C. (2023). *How trauma affects kids in school: Signs of trauma and tips for helping kids who've been traumatized.* Accessed at https://childmind.org/article/how-trauma-affects-kids-school on April 7, 2023.

Minero, E. (2017). *When students are traumatized, teachers are, too.* Accessed at www.edutopia.org/article/when-students-are-traumatized-teachers-are-too on July 15, 2023.

Moore, J. (2013). Research summary: Teaching and classroom strategies for homeless and highly mobile students. *National Center for Homeless Education.* Accessed at https://nche.ed.gov/wp-content/uploads/2018/11/res-summ-teach-class.pdf on August 2, 2023.

National Research Council and Institute of Medicine. (2010). *Student mobility: Exploring the impact of frequent moves on achievement: Summary of a workshop.* Washington, DC: National Academies Press.

Nesloney, T. (2018). *Stories from Webb: The ideas, passions, and convictions of a principal and his school family.* San Diego, CA: Dave Burgess Consulting, Inc.

Noguera, P. (2019, July 8). Equity isn't just a slogan. It should transform the way we educate kids [Blog post]. *The Holdsworth Center.* Accessed at https://holdsworthcenter.org/blog/equity-isnt-just-a-slogan on April 7, 2023.

Ondrasek, N., & Flook, L. (2020). How to help all students feel safe to be themselves. *Greater Good Magazine.* Accessed at https://greatergood.berkeley.edu/article/item/how_to_help_all_students_feel_safe_to_be_themselves on April 23, 2023.

O'Toole, C., & Dobutowitsch, M. (2022). The courage to care: Teacher compassion predicts more positive attitudes toward trauma-informed practice. *Journal of Child and Adolescent Trauma, 16,* 123–133.

Park, E., & Shin, M. (2020). A meta-analysis of special education teachers' burnout. *SAGE Open.* Accessed at https://journals.sagepub.com/doi/full/10.1177/2158244020918297 on July 17, 2023.

Pew Research Center. (2019). *Almost a quarter of U.S. children live in single-parent homes, more than in any other country.* Accessed at www.pewresearch.org/short-reads/2019/12/12/u-s-children-more-likely-than-children-in-other-countries-to-live-with-just-one-parent/ft_19-12-12_ussingleparents_map on May 15, 2023.

Poehler, A. (2011, May 25). *Amy Poehler at Harvard College class day* [Video file]. Accessed at www.youtube.com/watch?v=T7N_L_pu74k&t=13s on July 16, 2023.

Popp, P. A. (2014). *Tips for supporting mobile students.* Accessed at https://education.wm.edu/centers/hope/publications/infobriefs/documents/mobility2014.pdf on May 15, 2023.

Radd, S., Gooden, M. A., Generett, G. G., & Theoharis, G. (2022). *What if schools truly partnered with families living in poverty?* Accessed at www.ascd.org/el/articles/what-if-schools-truly-partnered on May 15, 2023.

Rakel, D. (2018). *The compassionate connection: The healing power of empathy and mindful listening.* New York: W.W. Norton & Company.

Rozin, P., & Royzman, E. B. (2001). Negativity bias, negativity dominance, and contagion [Abstract]. *Personality and Social Psychology Review.* Accessed at https://journals.sagepub.com/doi/10.1207/S15327957PSPR0504_2 on July 7, 2023.

Rumberger, R. W. (2015). *Student mobility: Causes, consequences, and solutions.* Accessed at https://files.eric.ed.gov/fulltext/ED574695.pdf on August 2, 2023.

Schwartz, K. (2016). *I wish my teacher knew: How one question can change everything for our kids.* Boston: Da Capo Lifelong Books.

Schweizer, A., Niedlich, S., Adamczyk, J., & Bormann, I. (2017). Approaching trust and control in parental relationships with educational institutions. *Studia Paedagogica, 22*(2), 97–115.

SHARE Team. (2012). How comfortable classrooms lead to better student community. *Resilient Educator*. Accessed at https://resilienteducator.com /classroom-resources/welcoming-classrooms-better-students on July 16, 2023.

Shaw, H. (2013). *Sticking points: How to get 4 generations working together in the 12 places they come apart*. Carol Stream, IL: Tyndale House Publishers.

Sheldon-Dean, H. (2022). 2022 children's mental health report: Treating symptoms of trauma in children and teenagers. *Child Mind Institute*. Accessed at https:// childmind.org/wp-content/uploads/2022/10/Trauma_Report_2022.pdf on August 7, 2023.

Smith School of Business. (2015). *Patricia Devine on kicking the prejudice habit* [Video file]. Accessed at www.youtube.com/watch?v=0OqRl3_m5WM on May 15, 2023.

Sparks, S. D. (2019). Why teacher-student relationships matter. *Education Week*. Accessed at www.edweek.org/teaching-learning/why-teacher-student -relationships-matter/2019/03 on July 16, 2023.

Srakocic, S. (2022). Why social and emotional learning is so important for kids right now. *Healthline*. Accessed at www.healthline.com/health/mental-health/social -emotional-learning-important on July 16, 2023.

Stamp, J., Frigon, C., Dupere, V., Dion, E., Oliver, E., & Archambault, I. (2022). School mobility and high school dropout: Seasonal and developmental timing matters. *Frontiers in Education, 7*.

Steele, D., & Whitaker, T. (2019). *Essential truths for principals*. New York: Routledge.

St. John, K., & Briel, L. (2017). Student voice: A growing movement within education that benefits students and teachers. *Virginia Commonwealth University Center on Transition Innovations*. Accessed at https://centerontransition.org /publications/download.cfm?id=61 on July 17, 2023.

Terziev, J. (2018, May 21). Family matters: The role of home visits in children's learning [Blog post]. *Institute of Educational Sciences*. Accessed at https://ies .ed.gov/ncee/rel/Products/Region/midatlantic/Blog/30187# on July 17, 2023.

Tischio, C. (2021). Compassion: A teacher's greatest learning tool. *ASCD, 17*(5). Accessed at www.ascd.org/el/articles/compassion-a-teachers-greatest-learning-tool on April 7, 2023.

Tough, P. (2016). Helping children succeed: What works and why. *Stanford Social Innovation Review*. Accessed at https://ssir.org/books/excerpts/entry/helping _children_succeed_what_works_and_why on April 19, 2023.

Tsipursky, G. (2020, July 13). What is unconscious bias (and how you can defeat it. [Blog post]. *Psychology Today*. Accessed at www.psychologytoday.com/us/blog /intentional-insights/202007/what-is-unconscious-bias-and-how-you-can-defeat-it on July 16, 2023.

United Nations Department of Economic and Social Affairs, Population Division. (2020). *International migration 2020 highlights*. Accessed at www.un.org /development/desa/pd/sites/www.un.org.development.desa.pd/files/undesa _pd_2020_international_migration_highlights.pdf on May 15, 2023.

University of Massachusetts Global. (n.d.). *Self-care for teachers: 5 strategies to prevent compassion fatigue* [Blog post]. Accessed at www.umassglobal.edu/news-and -events/blog/self-care-for-teachers on August 2, 2023.

Valcour, M. (2016). Beating burnout. *Harvard Business Review*. Accessed at https:// hbr.org/2016/11/beating-burnout on July 17, 2023.

Vazquez, A. (2022). How to mitigate your unconscious bias. *Gladstone Institutes*. Accessed at https://gladstone.org/news/how-mitigate-your-unconscious-bias on May 15, 2023.

Ventura, M. (2018). *Applied empathy: The new language of leadership*. New York: Touchstone.

Vesely, A., Saklofske, D., & Leschied, A. (2013). Teachers—The vital resource: The contribution of emotional intelligence to teacher efficacy and well-being. *Canadian Journal of Psychology, 28*(71), 71–89.

Wlodkowski, R. J. (1983). *Motivational opportunities for successful teaching: Leader's guide*. Phoenix, AZ: Universal Dimensions.

World Health Organization. (2019). *QD85 burnout: International Classification of Diseases*. Accessed at https://icd.who.int/browse11/l-m/en#/http://id.who.int/icd /entity/129180281 on July 17, 2023.

World Health Organization. (2022). *Violence against children*. Accessed at www.who .int/news-room/fact-sheets/detail/violence-against-children on July 15, 2023.

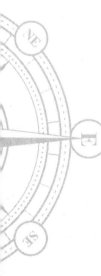

INDEX

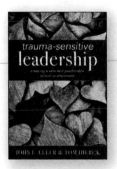

Trauma-Sensitive Leadership
John F. Eller and Tom Hierck
Lead a foundational shift in the way your school approaches student behavior. Using straightforward language, the authors offer research-based, practical strategies for understanding and supporting trauma-impacted students and providing a safe environment for them to learn.
BKF911

The Language of Possibility
Michael Roberts
Language can help lift or limit students. Based on brain research and authentic classroom experience, this book will help you get back to the optimism of teaching by connecting with the possibilities and gifts each student has to offer.
BKG048

Mindful School Communities
Christine Mason, Michele M. Rivers Murphy, and Yvette Jackson
Build a thriving school community that creates healthy, resilient, and successful students. A companion to *Mindfulness Practices*, this research-backed guide outlines how to teach self-regulation by fostering the five Cs of social and emotional learning and mindfulness: consciousness, compassion, confidence, courage, and community.
BKF912

EMPOWER Moves for Social-Emotional Learning
Lauren Porosoff and Jonathan Weinstein
Empower students to discover the values they want to live by. You will learn 28 activities, as well as extensions and variations for each, that engage students and help them make school a source of meaning, vitality, and community in their lives.
BKG095